official
motorcycling
CBT, theory & practical test

London: The Stationery Office

Published by The Stationery Office for the Driving Standards Agency under licence from the Controller of Her Majesty's Stationery Office

© Crown Copyright 2001

All rights reserved. Applications for reproduction should be made in writing to The Copyright Unit, Her Majesty's Stationery Office, St Clements House, 2–16 Colegate, Norwich NR3 1BQ

ISBN 011 552258 1

A CIP catalogue record for this book is available from the British Library

Other titles in the Driving Skills series

The Official Theory Test for Motorcyclists

The Official Theory Test for Car Drivers

The Official Theory Test for Drivers of Large Vehicles

Motorcycle Riding – The Essential Skills

The Official Driving Manual

The Official Driving Test

The Official Guide to Accompanying L-drivers

The Official Bus and Coach Driving Manual

The Official Goods Vehicle Driving Manual

The Official Tractor and Specialist Vehicle Driving Tests

The Official Theory Test and Beyond (CD-ROM)

The Official DSA Guide for Driving Instructors

Acknowledgments

The Driving Standards Agency (DSA) would like to thank the staff of the following organisations for their contribution to the production of this publication

Department of the Environment, Transport and the Regions.

Every effort has been made to ensure that the information contained in this publication is accurate at the time of going to press. The Stationery Office cannot be held responsible for any inaccuracies. Information in this book is for guidance only.

DSA CBT AND THE TEST

The Driving Standards Agency (DSA) is an executive agency of the Department of the Environment. Transport and the Regions.

You'll see its logo at test centres.

DSA aims to promote road safety through the advancement of driving standards by

- establishing and developing high standards and best practice in driving and riding on the road; before people start to drive, as they learn, and after they pass their test
- ensuring high standards of instruction for different types of driver and rider
- conducting the statutory theory and practical tests effeciently, fairly and consistently across the country
- providing a centre of excellence for driver training and driving standards
- develop a range of publications and other publicity material designed to promote safe driving for life.

DSA Website

www.driving-tests.co.uk

loo2279610

DSA CBT AND THE TEST

CONTENTS

PART FIVE   ## Retesting for disqualified riders

PART SIX   ## Further information

DSA CBT AND THE TEST

Over the years various pieces of legislation have been introduced to reduce two-wheeled motor vehicle casualties, including the compulsory wearing of safety helmets, restrictions on the size of learner motorcycles and most recently the requirement for all learner riders to pass a theory test.

Compulsory Basic Training (CBT) was introduced in 1990 to equip new riders with basic skills before riding unaccompanied on the road. CBT isn't a test and there's no exam – it's a course of training you're required to complete satisfactorily. As a road safety initiative it has proved to be a great success and motorcycling today is safer than it has ever been.

On the other hand the purpose of the practical test is to prove that you can ride your motorcycle safely on the road. During your practical test your examiner will want to see you riding to the standards set in this book. Those standards are given here in an easy-to-read style with illustrations, which explain simply what is required. However, riding is never predictable. Road conditions or circumstances will demand that you use your initiative or common sense. You should be able to assess any situation and apply the guidance given in this book.

You shouldn't assume that if you pass your tests you're a good rider with nothing more to learn. Learning to ride a motorcycle is a continuous process, and the tests are just one stage in your riding career.

Make sure that your aim is always *'Safe riding for life'*.

Robin Cummins
Chief Driving Examiner
Driving Standards Agency

This book will help you to

- understand the CBT course
- follow your progress through each element of the course
- learn to ride competently
- prepare for and pass your practical motorcycle test.

Part One outlines the modular content of CBT and tells you what you need to know about your motorcycle licence.

Part Two explains the details of each module of the CBT course.

Part Three contains advice on how to continue your training after CBT and tells you what you need to do before the test.

Part Four gives the test requirements, with simple, clear advice. Refer to it regularly when preparing for your test.

Part Five gives details about the extended test for disqualified riders.

Part Six gives other useful information including addresses which may be helpful. There is also a personal CBT training record which you can use to keep track of your progress through your CBT course.

The important factors

You're just beginning your motorcycling career and this book is only one of the important factors in your training. Others are

- a good instructor
- a positive attitude
- patience and practice.

How you choose to develop as a motorcyclist is up to you. You should aim to be a safe and confident rider for life. Don't just put on a show for your test and then revert to a lower standard. Take pride in always setting a good example.

Riding safely is a life skill.

Books for study

It's strongly recommended that you study a copy of *The Highway Code* (The Stationery Office). You can buy a copy from all good booksellers.

The DSA 'Driving Skills' series of books will provide you with sound knowledge of riding skills and safe riding practices. *The Official Theory Test for Motorcyclists* and *The Official Motorcycling Manual* are both published by The Stationery Office.

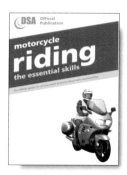

The topics covered

- What is CBT?
- The CBT course
- Approved Training Bodies
- Your motorcycle licence.

What is CBT?

CBT is a course of compulsory basic training which all learner motorcycle and moped riders must complete before riding on the road.

In addition, holders of a full car licence obtained by passing their driving test on or after 1 February 2001, must complete a CBT course if they wish to validate the full moped entitlement on their driving licence.

CBT can only be given by Approved Training Bodies (ATBs) who have

*   instructors that have been assessed by DSA
*   sites approved by DSA for off-road training.

CBT allows you to learn the following in a safe environment

*   motorcycling theory
*   skills which will make you safe on the road
*   the correct attitude towards motorcycling.

Many people find CBT is an enjoyable activity and an opportunity to meet like-minded motorcyclists.

You don't have to take CBT if you

*   have a full moped licence obtained by passing a moped test after 1 December 1990
*   already hold a valid CBT Certificate of Completion (DL196) obtained during a previous motorcycle entitlement or when riding a moped
*   hold a full motorcycle licence for one category and wish to upgrade to another.
*   live and ride on specified offshore islands

Certificate of Completion (DL196)

When you complete a CBT course you'll be given a Certificate of Completion of an Approved Training Course (DL196).

From 1 February 2001 the DL 196 will record whether CBT was completed on

- a moped or motorcycle
- a motorcycle-sidecar combination or moped that has more than 2 wheels

and will validate your entitlement accordingly.

Certificate life   From 1 February 2001 CBT certificates have a two-year life.

Certificates issued before that date will remain valid for the remainder of their three year life.

A Certificate validating full moped entitlement on a full car licence will remain valid for mopeds, for the life of the licence.

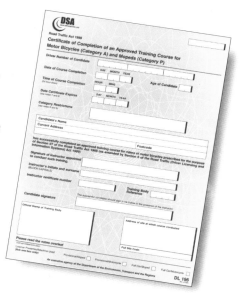

Note

If training is completed on a motorcycle-sidecar combination or on a moped that has more than 2 wheels

- moped validation will be limited to mopeds with more than 2 wheels
- motorcycle validation will be limited to motorcycle-sidecar combinations.

The CBT course

CBT is arranged so that you progress through a series of elements. You will only move onto the next element when your instructor is satisfied you

- have learnt the necessary theory
- have demonstrated the practical skills to a safe basic level.

The elements are

- 'A' Introduction
- 'B' Practical on-site training
- 'C' Practical on-site riding
- 'D' Practical on-road training
- 'E' Practical on-road riding.

The elements are described in detail in Part Two.

Element order

The elements MUST be taken in the order shown. Your instructor will ensure you complete each element before you progress to the next.

Within each element the instructor is free to deliver the training in the order which is felt to be most appropriate for you.

The CBT record in Part Six of this book will allow you to record when each of the elements has been completed.

Instructor-to-trainee ratios

During your CBT you may be accompanied by other learners up to a maximum ratio of

- 4:1 during on-site elements
- 2:1 during the on-road element.

For those using the Direct Access scheme (see page 8) the ratios are 2:1 for both on- and off-road elements.

Approved Training Bodies

CBT can only be given by ATBs using instructors who are either

- DSA Assessed Certified Instructors or
- Down-Trained Certified Instructors or
- Assistant Instructors.

DSA Assessed Certified Instructors

Every ATB must employ at least one instructor who has successfully attended DSA's CBT assessment. They're called Cardington Assessed Instructors and can

- provide CBT training and issue DL196 certificates
- down-train other instructors within the ATB.

Down-Trained Certified Instructors

These instructors have been down-trained by the Cardington Assessed Instructor and are qualified to provide CBT training including issuing the DL196 certificate at the end of the course.

Assistant Instructors

An Assistant Instructor can deliver the off-road training elements, but is not entitled to carry out any on-road training or issue DL196 certificates.

Direct Access supervision

Some instructors may have a further qualification allowing them to give Direct Access supervision. This is obtained by attending DSA's Direct Access Scheme assessment.

How can I tell which type of instructor is giving me training?

When training your instructor will be carrying with them their certificate. A certificate containing the letter C indicates a Cardington Assessed Instructor while a D indicates they are Direct Access qualified. Some certificates contain both qualifications.

Quality control

DSA monitors the standard of training given by instructors. If a DSA examiner is present during your training. don't worry. The examiner

- will not take part in the training
- is there to safeguard the quality of training you receive.

Choosing an ATB

You can find out about the ATBs in your area from

- the local road safety officer
- most motorcycle dealers
- motorcycle papers and magazines
- local papers
- Yellow Pages
- DSA tel: 0115 901 2500.

Hiring a motorcycle

ATBs usually have motorcycles you can hire for

- CBT
- additional training
- your practical test.

These may be

- learner rated motorcycles
- Direct Access rated motorcycles.

Talk to local ATBs to find out what they can offer.

If you hire equipment and the machine from the ATB they should provide the necessary insurance.

Clothing

Your instructor will discuss motorcycle clothing in detail as part of the CBT course.

If you are just starting to ride it will pay you to listen to your instructor before rushing out to buy anything.

During your CBT course you

- must wear the visibility aid provided by the ATB. This will carry the name of the training organisation
- should wear appropriate clothing and stout footwear.

Many ATBs provide basic equipment for the CBT course.

See Element A (page 14).

Your motorcycle licence

To begin riding a motorcycle on the road you must be at least 17 years old and hold a driving licence which allows you to ride motorcycles (Category A).

That licence can be any of the following

- a provisional driving licence. This provides provisional car, motorcycle and moped entitlement
- full car licence. This provides provisional motorcycle entitlement
- a full moped licence. This provides provisional motorcycle entitlement.

All riders must

- wear a saftey helmet at all times when riding unless they are a member of the Sikh religion and wear a turban
- ensure any helmet visor used conforms to BSI standards.

Note

From 1 February 2001 provisional driving licences will be issued with provisional motorcycle entitlement valid for the life of the licence (subject to holding a valid CBT certificate).

Provisional motorcycle licences issued before 1 February 2001 required the practical motorcycle test to be passed within 2 years of the date of issue or motorcycle entitlement would be withdrawn for 1 year. From 1 February 2001 these licence holders may

- apply for a replacement licence at the end of 2 years without a 12-month waiting period. The replacement licence will be issued until age 70.

- apply for a replacement licence immediately if the licence has already expired under the 2-year rule. The replacement licence will be issued until age 70.
- apply for a replacement licence immediately if the licence has been surrendered to preserve the balance of the 2 years. The replacement licence will be issued until age 70.

Driving licence application forms are available from

- Post Offices
- Traffic Area Offices
- Vehicle Registration Offices
- Driver and Vehicle Licensing Agency (DVLA).

Provisional motorcycle entitlement

After completing CBT learners may ride a solo motorcycle

- up to 125 cc
- with a power output of no more than 11 kW.

Learners who wish to ride a sidecar outfit can do so as long as it has a power-to-weight ratio not exceeding 0.16 kW/kg.

With provisional motorcycle entitlement you must not

- ride on motorways
- carry a pillion passenger
- ride without red L-plates fitted to both front and rear of the motorcycle. In Wales you may display red D-plates (for *dysgwr*, the Welsh for learner). If you cross from Wales into another part of the United Kingdom you must display L-plates.

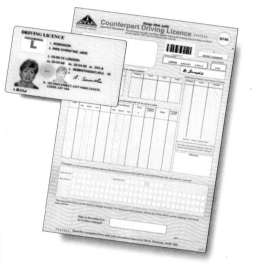

Theory Test

From 1 February 2001 all candidates for a practical motorcycle test must first pass a motorcycle theory test, unless

- upgrading from A1 to A
- a full moped licence is held which was obtained by passing the moped test after July 1996.

See Part three.

Full motorcycle licence

There are two types of full motorcycle licence

- Sub-category A1-Light Motorcycle licence
- Category A-Standard Motorcycle licence.

Sub-category A1

A full A1 licence allows you to ride machines up to 125 cc and with a power output of up to 11 kW (14.6 bhp).

You can obtain a full sub-category A1 licence by passing the practical test on a bike of between 75 cc and 125 cc.

Category A

A full category A licence gives you full entitlement to all machines.

You can obtain a full category A licence

- with a two year qualifying period
- without a two year qualifying period via Direct Access.

Category A with 2 year qualifying period

This will be obtained by passing the motorcycle test on a motorcycle of between 121 cc and 125 cc and capable of at least 100 kph (62.5 mph).

Riders who are subject to the two year qualifying period will be restricted to machines of 25 kW (33 bhp) maximum or power to weight ratio not exceeding 0.16 kW/kg for two years from the date of passing their test. At the end of that time any size of motorcycle may be ridden without taking another test.

Category A via Direct Access

This is for riders aged 21 or over. Passing the motorcycle test on a machine of at least 35 kW (46.6 bhp) gives immediate access to all sizes of motorcycle.

You can practise on any size of motorcycle which exceeds the UK learner specification provided that

- you are accompanied at all times by a qualified approved instructor, on another motorcycle and in radio contact
- fluorescent or reflective safety clothing is worn during supervision
- L-plates (D-plates in Wales) are fitted and provisional licence restrictions followed.

Accelerated Access This option is for riders over 21 years old or who reach the age of 21 before their two-year qualifying period is complete.

You can take a further test to give you immediate access to all motorcycles. This test must be taken on a motorcycle with a power output of at least 35 kW (46.6 bhp).

You can practise for this test on motorcycles above 25 kW (33 bhp) provided

- you're accompanied at all times by an approved instructor, on another motorcycle and in radio contact
- fluorescent or reflective safety clothing is worn during supervision
- L-plates (or D-plates in Wales) are fitted and provisional licence restrictions followed.

Full licence entitlement

With a full motorcycle licence you may

- ride without L-plates (or D-plates in Wales)
- carry a pillion passenger
- use motorways.

Moped riders

To ride a moped on the road you must be at least 16 years old and have a driving licence that entitles you to ride mopeds (Category P).

At 16 but under 17 this can be a

* full moped licence
* provisional moped licence.

At 17 and over it can also be a

* full car licence (see below)
* full motorcycle licence
* provisional driving licence. This provides provisional moped entitlement.

Provisional moped entitlement

After completing CBT this allows you to ride a moped. You must not

* carry a pillion passenger
* ride without red L-plates (or D-plates in Wales) fitted to both the front and the rear of the moped
* ride on the motorways.

Full moped licence

Full moped entitlement allows you to

* ride mopeds without L-plates
* carry a pillion passenger.

Remember Mopeds are not allowed on motorways, even if you hold a full licence.

Full car licence holders

Holders of a full car licence obtained by passing their driving test before 1 February 2001 hold unconditional full moped entitlement.

Holders of a full car licence obtained by passing their driving test on or after 1 February 2001, who do not already hold a full moped or motorcycle licence, must hold a valid DL196 to validate their full moped entitlement.

If a valid DL196 is already held when the car test is passed, the full moped entitlement will be validated immediately.

A DL196 validating full moped entitlement on a full car licence will remain valid for mopeds, for the life of the licence. It is therefore particularly important that the DL196 is kept safe.

Remember The same DL196 that validates your full moped entitlement will have a limited life (see Certificate life) for validating provisional motorcycle entitlement.

Mopeds

* have an engine under 50 cc
* have a maximum design speed not exceeding 50 kph (31 mph)
* don't weigh more than 250 kg
* can be moved by pedals if the moped was registered before 1 August 1977.

PART TWO CBT

INTRODUCTION TO CBT

The topics covered

- The aims of CBT
- Equipment and clothing
- Eyesight test.

The aims of Element A

This element is an introduction to CBT.

It will take the form of a discussion. Your instructor will explain the basics and not get involved in complicated issues.

Wherever possible your instructor will use examples to help demonstrate the point being made.

As a part of this element you'll have your entitlement to ride motorcycles checked. If necessary your instructor will explain what you need to do in order to obtain this entitlement.

At the end of this module you should understand the

- purpose of CBT
- content of CBT.

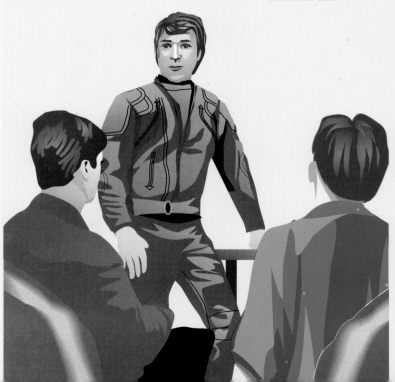

What CBT requires

You cannot ride on the road until you have satisfactorily completed all the elements of CBT.

Your instructor will explain the aims of CBT and will also explain why it was introduced.

An overview of the course content should be given.

The time it takes to complete the course will be determined by you. Your instructor should not move you on to the next part until you're ready.

Within each element instructors are free to deliver the topics in the order that they find best for you. Every topic must, however, be covered to the necessary level.

You'll need to demonstrate to your instructor that you have a basic skill level and an understanding of each topic. This may be through question and answer sessions for the theory or through practical demonstrations of your riding ability.

Points to remember

Don't treat CBT as a formality you must grudgingly endure.

Instructors are experienced motorcyclists who

• have valuable advice to give learner riders
• are motorcycle enthusiasts.

Take CBT seriously and enjoy learning safely.

Many experienced car drivers who take up motorcycling, find that CBT is an eye opening experience which

• increases their awareness of hazards
• gives them skills which improve their driving.

Element A

What CBT requires

Your instructor will explain the different types of motorcycle clothing available. As well as looking at outer clothing, the talk will include

- helmets
- visors and goggles
- gloves
- boots.

Motorcycle equipment is generally expensive and your instructor will help

- prioritise which equipment you should buy first
- identify less expensive alternatives.

You should also discuss

- the effects of getting cold and wet
- how some clothing can help protect from certain injuries.

Points to remember

You'll need to know

- the legal requirements for helmets
- how to fasten your helmet securely
- about the BSI Kitemark on visors and goggles.

You must also know the dangers of riding

- with scratched, damaged and tinted visors or goggles
- with a damaged helmet
- without eye protection
- without gloves
- in shorts
- in sandals or trainers
- without adequate clothing in bad weather.

What CBT requires

At this stage in CBT your instructor will check your eyesight.

You must be able to read a number plate

- in good daylight
- with letters 79.4 mm (3.1 in) high
- at a distance of 20.5 m (about 67 feet)
- with the aid of glasses or contact lenses if necessary.

When number plates with the narrower font are introduced the minimum distance will be 20 m (about 66 feet).

Points to remember

If you fail to reach the required standard in the eyesight test, the remaining elements of the course cannot proceed.

You **must** demonstrate that you can reach the required eyesight standard, using glasses or contact lenses if necessary, before further elements can be taken.

If you've demonstrated that you need to wear glasses or contact lenses to pass the eyesight test, you **must** wear them for the rest of the course and whenever you ride on the road.

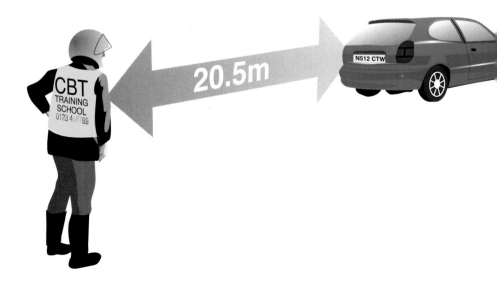

PRACTICAL ON-SITE TRAINING

The topics covered

- Motorcycles and their controls
- Basic safety checks and use of the stands
- Wheeling the motorcycle and braking to stop
- Starting and stopping the engine.

The aims of Element B

This element provides you with an introduction to the motorcycle.

You'll not start riding the motorcycle in this element although you'll get hands-on training.

At the end of the element you'll

- be able to show a working knowledge of the machine
- have a feel for the weight and balance of a motorcycle.

INSTRUCTOR

L

What CBT requires

Your instructor will show you around a motorcycle and will explain the controls in a logical order.

The controls covered will include

- hand controls
- foot controls
- instruments.

Hand controls

- throttle
- front brake
- clutch
- indicators
- choke
- electric starter
- engine cut-off or kill switch
- lighting switches
- horn
- fuel tap.

Foot controls

- rear brake
- kick starter
- gear change lever.

Instruments

- speedometer
- rev counter
- warning lamps
- water temperature and fuel gauges.

Skills you'll acquire

Practise finding and using the controls. Some controls are adjustable. Your instructor will explain how they can be set up to suit you.

You'll also need to develop a feel for the controls. Remember that when riding you'll be wearing gloves and boots. This may affect the feel and ease with which you can reach certain controls.

Faults to avoid

It should not require great strength or force to operate the motorcycle's controls. Be especially careful with

- throttle
- clutch
- brakes.

You must be able to operate the controls smoothly and without having to look down to find them.

Element B

What CBT requires

Your instructor will show you how to make basic checks to ensure your motorcycle is safe.

These checks will include

- the brakes for correct operation and adjustment
- the steering head for wear and adjustment
- control cables for wear, adjustment and lubrication
- fluid levels
  - hydraulic brake fluid
  - engine oil
  - coolant
  - battery electrolyte
- all lights
- suspension
- wheels and spokes
- tyres for wear, damage and pressure
- drive chain for wear, lubrication and tension
- nuts and bolts for tightness
- number plate and reflectors for visibility
- mirrors for clarity.

You will also be shown the types of motorcycle stands and how and when to use them.

Skills you'll acquire

While you're not expected to become a motorcycle mechanic, you'll need to be able to recognise basic faults which could affect your motorcycle's roadworthiness.

When using the stands you need to

- demonstrate the correct techniques for putting a motorcycle onto and off its stands
- show an understanding of the effects of camber and gradient.

Faults to avoid

It's important that you know which machine checks you need to make on a daily basis and which can be left longer.

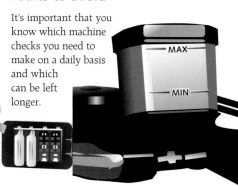

Make sure you can manage using the stands correctly. Incorrect methods of using the stands can lead to personal injury or damage to the machine.

What CBT requires

You'll learn how to balance a motorcycle while wheeling it both to the left and right (in either order).

Your instructor will show you

- where to stand
- how to hold the motorcycle
- how to lean the motorcycle while wheeling it.

In addition you'll be taught how to use the front brake to stop in a controlled manner. This will involve

- making sure the motorcycle is upright
- practice to get the feel of the front brake.

Skills you'll acquire

You'll have to demonstrate

- full control of the motorcycle while wheeling it
- that you have the necessary balance skills.

Your instructor will want to see that you can squeeze the front brake gently and effectively to stop.

Faults to avoid

When wheeling the motorcycle, avoid

- holding somewhere other than the handlebar grips
- wobbling
- insecure control
- looking down
- harsh use of the front brake.

What CBT requires

Your instructor will show you what checks you need to make before starting the engine. A mnemonic such as FIGS may be used.

Fuel   You'll be shown how to

- check for fuel in the tank
- turn on the fuel tap
- use the reserve position.

The use of the choke will also be explained.

Ignition   You'll be shown

- the positions on the ignition switch
- how to switch on the ignition.

The engine kill switch will be explained.

Gears   This will cover checking for neutral by

- checking the neutral lamp
- rocking the machine back and forward
- spinning the rear wheel on the stand.

Start   You should be shown how to use

- electric starters
- kick starters.

Skills you'll acquire

Before starting the engine you'll need to

- be able to find neutral and recognise a 'false neutral'
- demonstrate that you know how to operate the ignition switch and any immobiliser fitted
- know how to operate the starter mechanism fitted to your machine.

Faults to avoid

Before you start the engine don't forget to turn on the fuel. The engine may well start but will splutter and cut out before you've travelled far if you don't.

Only use the choke for the shortest period necessary. Running with the choke on for longer than you need to can cause

- the engine to run too fast when you're trying to slow down
- increased wear on the engine
- more fuel to be used and more pollution produced.

When starting the engine

- make sure you have selected neutral
- don't hold the kick start lever down after the kick over
- don't hold the starter button on after the engine has started.

When stopping the engine don't

- use the kill switch unless in an emergency
- forget to switch off the fuel tap.

PRACTICAL ON-SITE RIDING

The topics covered

- Riding in a straight line and stopping
- Riding slowly
- Using the brakes
- Changing gear
- Riding a figure of eight
- Emergency stopping
- Rear observation
- Turning left and right
- U-turn.

The aims of Element C

In this element you'll begin riding a motorcycle.

By the time you've finished this element you'll have developed enough basic skills to allow you to ride a motorcycle under control.

You'll also learn the essential techniques you need for dealing with hazards including

- rear observation
- Observation–Signal–Manoeuvre (OSM) and Position– Speed–Look (PSL) routines.

You will practise these practical skills until your instructor is satisfied that you'll be safe when you're taken out onto the road.

What CBT requires

This is the point in CBT where you begin riding a motorcycle.

Your instructor will explain and may also demonstrate what's required.

You'll be shown how to move off and how to stop. This will include

- using the clutch
- selecting first gear
- finding the 'biting point'
- using the brakes to stop.

Covering the rear brake will be explained to you and you'll be expected to put this into practice.

Your instructor will also show you how to ride in a straight line, including advice on how to keep your balance.

Skills you'll acquire

You'll need to practise until you can

- coordinate the controls when moving off and stopping
- keep your balance
- use both brakes in a smooth and controlled manner.

Faults to avoid

When you move off for the first time you may feel insecure. Avoid riding with your feet hanging down. From the beginning learn to ride with your feet up on the footrests.

When you stop you'll have to put a foot down to support the motorcycle. Your instructor will explain

- which foot to put down
- why that foot.

Follow the guidance and make sure you understand why.

Avoid fierce use of the controls at all times as this can lead to

- stalling the engine
- skidding
- loss of steering control.

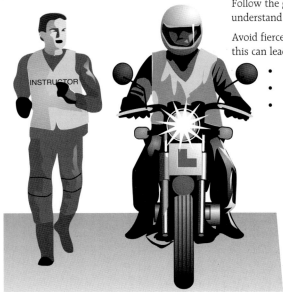

Element

C

What CBT requires

You'll have to show you can ride a motorcycle slowly and under full control. This is to prepare you for riding on the road where this skill will be needed to deal with

- junctions
- slow moving traffic in queues
- hazards.

A demonstration of what is required will probably be given to help show

- the level of control achievable
- how slowly you'll be expected to ride.

Skills you'll acquire

You'll need to demonstrate your skill in using the

- throttle
- clutch
- brakes

while keeping your

- balance
- steering

under control.

Faults to avoid

- loss of balance
- loss of steering control
- harsh use of
  - throttle
  - clutch
  - brakes
- riding too fast
- not using the footrests.

DSA **CBT AND THE TEST**

What CBT requires

You need to be able to operate the brakes in a controlled manner so that you can

- control your speed
- stop accurately.

You'll be shown how to use both brakes together for maximum control and stopping ability.

The importance of this skill can be related to the need to stop accurately at junctions.

Skills you'll acquire

Your instructor will expect you to stop the motorcycle at a marked position.

Cones, a line or some other marker may be used to identify where you are expected to stop.

Faults to avoid

- Not de-clutching as you stop.
- Use of the rear brake before the front.
- Use of one brake only.
- Harsh and late use of the brakes.
- Locking the wheels.

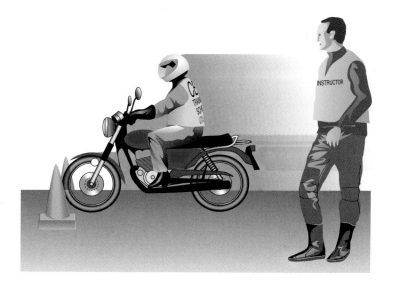

What CBT requires

You need to be able to change up and down smoothly through the gears.

Your instructor will explain how to operate the controls to achieve smooth gear changes.

The space on the training area may limit practice to second or third gear.

Skills you'll acquire

You'll need to demonstrate that you can

- coordinate the controls
- make upward and downward gear changes satisfactorily.

Faults to avoid

- harsh use of the controls
- failing to co-ordinate clutch, throttle and gear change lever
- selecting the wrong gear.

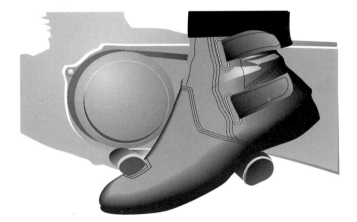

What CBT requires

This exercise is to develop steering and balance control when changing from one lock to another.

There are no set size measurements for this exercise. Your instructor may start off with a large layout and reduce it as your skill develops.

Skills you'll acquire

You will learn

- precise throttle and clutch control
- slow speed steering and balance control.

Faults to avoid

- riding with your feet off the footrests
- harsh throttle and clutch control
- excessive speed
- wobbling.

Element C

What CBT requires

You must be able to stop safely should an emergency arise.

Your instructor will explain the effects of

- using the brakes individually
- using both brakes together.

This may then be followed by a demonstration to highlight the points.

You need to understand

- how weight is transferred during heavy braking
- how weight transfer can affect the rear wheel.

Reference may be made to using the brakes in the ratio 75% front and 25% rear. It's important to understand that this refers to braking force, not lever movement.

The effects of weather conditions on this ratio will also need to be explained.

Skills you'll acquire

You must be able to coordinate front and rear brakes

- together
- in the correct ratio for the conditions.

Faults to avoid

- late reactions when signalled to stop
- excessive brake pressure causing either or both wheels to lock
- not responding to the weather and road conditions
- not de-clutching as you stop.

What CBT requires

To be safe on the road you should know as much about the traffic behind as you can.

On a motorcycle you can find out about traffic behind by

- using the mirrors
- turning and looking over your shoulder.

Your instructor will explain the special requirements for a motorcyclist including

- how and when to use mirrors
- how to overcome the blind area.

You should practise looking round

- before moving off
- whilst on the move.

Skills you'll acquire

You'll need to practise looking round while moving so that

- you can see into the blind area
- you learn to keep control whilst looking round.

Faults to avoid

- looking round for an excessive time
- veering off course while looking round
- poorly timed rearward glances.

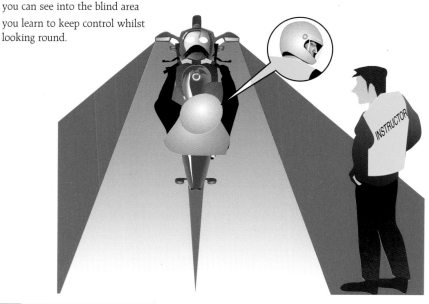

What CBT requires

You need to be able to deal safely with road junctions. Your instructor will explain the

- Observation
- Signal
- Manoeuvre
- Position
- Speed
- Look

procedure (**OSM/PSL**) and may give a demonstration.

The 'lifesaver' look will be explained.

An explanation of

- different junction types
- road markings
- traffic signals and signs

will be given.

You will need to know how to deal with left and right turns

- minor to major
- major to minor.

A mock junction layout may be set out on the training area for practice.

Skills you'll acquire

Right and left turns require different procedures. You need to

- recognise the different types of turn
- demonstrate correct road positioning
- make effective observation
- give correct signals in good time.

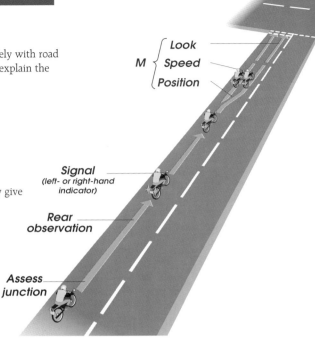

Look
M { *Speed*
Position

Signal
(left- or right-hand indicator)

Rear observation

Assess junction

Faults to avoid

- making badly timed rearward or sideways glances
- giving badly timed or incorrect signals
- looking around when the situation calls for concentration ahead
- not cancelling signals after turning.

What CBT requires

Riding a U-turn is a set exercise which also has practical use when riding on the road.

You need to be able to ride your motorcycle around in a U-turn

- under control
- with your feet on the footrests
- keeping aware of the traffic conditions.

Your instructor may demonstrate the level of

- balance
- steering
- clutch/throttle

control needed for this exercise.

You'll be given the chance to practise until you're confident of your ability.

Skills you'll acquire

To ride around in a U-turn you need to have developed your

- balance
- steering
- clutch/throttle

coordination and control.

In addition you need to understand

- when
- how
- where

to look for traffic or other hazards.

Faults to avoid

- harsh use of the controls
- not taking effective observation
- using your feet to help overcome poor balance.

PRACTICAL ON-ROAD TRAINING

The topics covered

- Conspicuity
- Legal requirements
- Vulnerability
- Speed
- *Highway Code*
- Anticipation
- Rear observation
- Road positioning
- Separation distance
- Weather conditions
- Road surfaces
- Alcohol and drugs
- Attitude
- Hazard perception.

The aims of Element D

Having carried out theory and practical training off-road, your instructor will now prepare you for the on-road element of CBT.

The knowledge you gain now will be the foundations on which to build your motorcycling career.

This element will cover the information you need to ride

- legally
- safely

on the road.

During Element E aspects of this theory may be reinforced in practical situations.

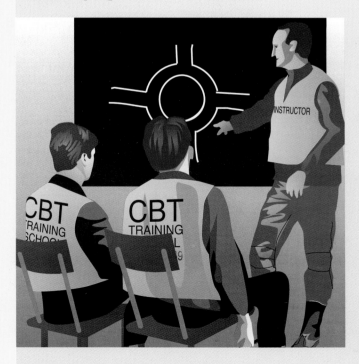

What CBT requires

It is vitally important to understand why you need to be conspicuous when riding a motorcycle.

Your instructor will discuss the reasons for not being seen and how you can make it easy for others to see you

The talk will include

- visibility aids
- differences between
    - fluorescent materials
    - reflective materials
- use of headlights
- road positioning
- clothing
- keeping your motorcycle clean.

This may be illustrated by a short video presentation.

In addition there will be some discussion on the legal requirements to use dipped headlights in poor visibility.

Points to remember

Making yourself conspicuous is not a legal requirement. However it's in your own interest to make yourself easy to see. To do so, avoid

- wearing dull clothing
- riding a dirty motorcycle
- riding in another road user's blind area.

Element
D

What CBT requires

Before you ride on the road there are minimum legal requirements you must be aware of.

Your instructor will explain about

- road tax
- insurance
- MOT certificates
- provisional motorcycle licence entitlement
- DL196 (CBT completion certificate)
- L-plates.

In addition you need to know about

- general roadworthiness
- the legal requirement to fasten your helmet correctly.

Points to remember

Make sure you have all the legal aspects in order before riding on the road. You'll not always be sent a reminder when certain mandatory items need renewal or expire such as

- MOT certificates
- DL196 certificates.

Don't get caught out through neglecting to keep everything up to date.

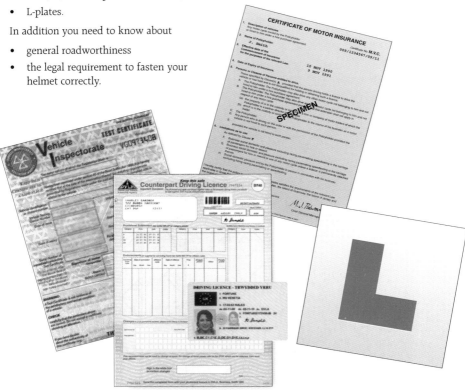

What CBT requires

As a motorcyclist you're generally more vulnerable than motorists.

Your instructor will explain about the dangers of

- falling off
- collision, even at low speed
- weather conditions
- road surface conditions.

The head and limbs are the most exposed parts of your body when riding. Your instructor will tell you what steps you can take to protect yourself from injury and the effects of the weather.

Points to remember

Always buy the best protective equipment you can afford.

Don't

- use a helmet that is
  - damaged
  - second hand
  - poor fitting
  - unfastened
- ride without protective clothing
- ride too fast for the conditions.

Element D

What CBT requires

You need to understand why riding at the correct speed is so important.

Riding too slowly can be just as much a problem as riding too fast.

Your instructor will explain about the

- legal speed limits
- suitable use of speed
- consequences of
  - speeding
  - riding too slowly.

Points to remember

You need to develop a defensive riding style so that you can always stop

- within your range of vision
- in case a potential hazard turns into a real danger.

Always ride within

- speed limits
- your ability.

What CBT requires

As a road user you should own a current copy of *The Highway Code* and refer to it often.

Without knowledge of *The Highway Code* you will find it difficult to deal with all aspects of training.

While *The Highway Code* contains **all** the essential elements of road safety, specific elements relating to CBT will be covered in more detail by your instructor.

Points to remember

Don't treat *The Highway Code* as a book to learn just for your driving test. It contains a wealth of information and advice which is designed to keep you safe whenever you use the road.

Refer to it often and follow the advice it gives.

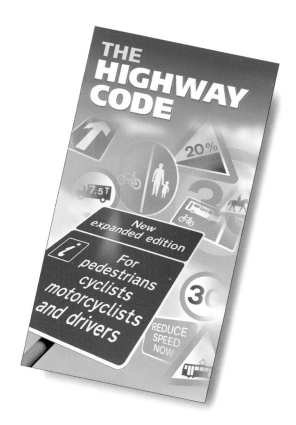

Element D

What CBT requires

At all times you should ride defensively and anticipate the actions of other road users.

Your instructor will explain that to anticipate you need to

- look well ahead
- plan ahead
- develop hazard awareness
- concentrate at all times.

During discussion your instructor will cover a variety of scenarios which illustrate the point being made.

Points to remember

Anticipation is a skill which develops over time. Signs which show a lack of anticipation include

- late and harsh braking
- being distracted
- not taking road and weather conditions into account.

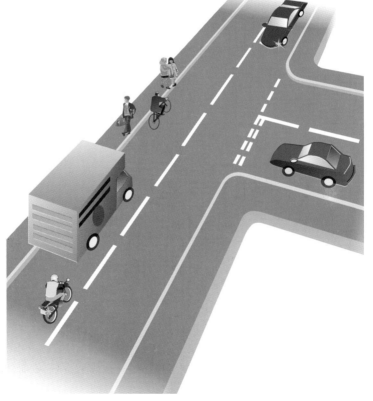

What CBT requires

You must understand that rear observation is a combination of

- using the mirrors
- looking around.

Your instructor will explain about

- effective rear observation
- timing of rearward glances
- 'lifesaver' checks.

Some time may be spent discussing the effects of looking around at the wrong moment.

Points to remember

Take care not to

- veer off course while looking round
- look round too late
- look round when you should be concentrating ahead.

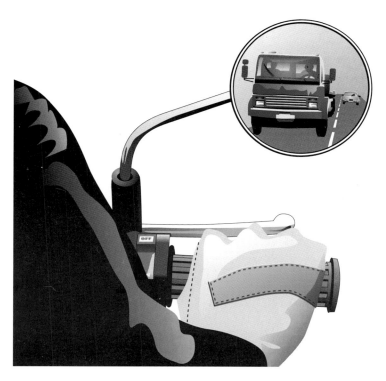

Element D

What CBT requires

It's important that you understand where you should position yourself when riding on the road.

Points which will be covered include how you should position yourself to deal with

- bends
- junctions
- road conditions
- single and dual carriageways
- hazards
- overtaking.

Points to remember

When you ride on the road always concentrate and avoid

- riding in the gutter
- erratic steering and veering across your lane
- failing to return to your normal position after dealing with a hazard
- riding on the crown of the road as a normal position.

DSA **CBT AND THE TEST**

What CBT requires

You must understand the importance of leaving sufficient space when following another vehicle.

This will involve discussing the advantages of allowing plenty of space such as

- increased ability to see past vehicles ahead and so allow for better forward planning
- increased likelihood of being seen by other road users.

The 'two-second rule' will be explained, and how this is affected by road and weather conditions should be covered.

The special advice for following large vehicles will also be discussed.

Points to remember

Always keep the correct separation distance from the vehicle ahead.

It's important to allow for the

- effect road and weather conditions have on your stopping distance
- blind area of large vehicles.

2 secs

B

1 sec

'Only a fool breaks the two-second rule'

start

A

B is too close to the car in front

Element
D

What CBT requires

Motorcyclists are affected more by weather conditions than most other road users.

You can expect some discussion on how

- wind
- rain
- fog
- ice
- snow and sleet

affect motorcyclists.

In addition your instructor will explain how these weather conditions affect

- oil spillage
- painted road markings
- drain covers.

There should be discussion on turbulence caused by large vehicles and the effect that buffeting can have on motorcyclists.

Points to remember

During your training you are unlikely to encounter severe bad weather conditions.

When you do find yourself having to ride in bad weather conditions remember the advice your instructor has given.

Always respect the effects weather can have when you're riding a motorcycle.

If in doubt, don't set out !

What CBT requires

You need to be aware of how road conditions can affect a motorcyclist.

There are a variety of road surface hazards which will be explained including

- mud and leaves
- gravel and chippings
- tram and railway lines
- studs
- road markings
- drain covers
- shiny surfaces at junctions and roundabouts.

Clues which can help new riders will be discussed, such as

- rainbow colourings on a wet road indicating oil or fuel spillage
- 'Loose chippings' road signs
- mud near farm and field entrances.

Points to remember

When you're riding always take the road conditions into account, especially when

- cornering
- accelerating
- braking.

What CBT requires

Alcohol

You are required to know that it's a criminal offence to ride with more than the legal level of alcohol in your blood.

Your instructor will make it clear that despite legally accepted limits, if you want to be safe and you're going to ride

DON'T DRINK AT ALL

Drugs

Taking certain drugs when you are going to ride is a criminal offence.

Your instructor will cover

- the effect drugs can have on concentration
- over the counter medicines
- how to check whether any medication will affect your riding ability
- how insurance policies could be invalidated.

Points to remember

Always

Avoid riding when under the influence of alcohol and/or drugs.

The effects could be **FATAL**

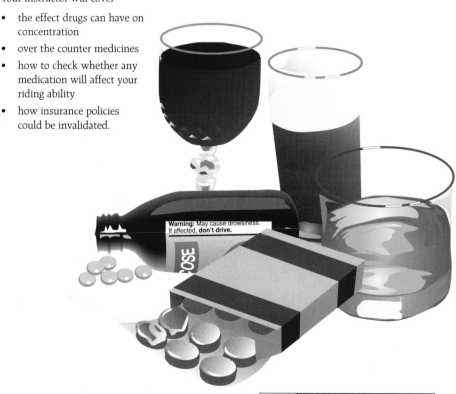

Warning: May cause drowsiness.
If affected, **don't drive.**

What CBT requires

Your instructor will explain how your attitude can affect your safety. The points raised should include the

- effects of riding while angry
- importance of showing patience
- benefits of riding defensively.

Points to remember

Your attitude is under your control. You could put yourself at additional risk by

- riding while upset or angry
- riding in a spirit of competition on the road
- giving offence or provoking reaction by creating dangerous situations.

Element D

What CBT requires

You will be given some idea of what is meant by a hazard.

Your instructor will explain

- the importance of planning ahead
- how early recognition makes hazards easier to deal with
- the need for concentration
- the need to use all your senses
- the importance controlling speed has in dealing with hazards.

Points to remember

Always keep up to date with the constantly changing road and traffic situations by

- concentrating at all times
- looking well ahead.

PRACTICAL ON-ROAD RIDING

The topics covered

- Traffic lights
- Roundabouts
- Junctions
- Pedestrian crossings
- Gradients
- Bends
- Obstructions
- U-turn
- Stopping as in an emergency.

The aims of Element E

This is the final element of the CBT course.

You'll ride out on the road

- accompanied by and in radio contact with a certified instructor*
- possibly with one other trainee
- for at least two hours.

You'll have to demonstrate that you can cope safely with a variety of road and traffic conditions.

Expect your instructor to stop now and again to

- discuss some aspect of your riding
- explain how to put the theory into practice.

Your ride should cover the topics discussed in this part of the book. (Some may not be covered because of the limits of the location.)

Your riding will be constantly assessed by your instructor, who will sign a certificate of completion (DL196) when satisfied you're safe to continue learning alone.

* Those who are profoundly deaf are exempt from the requirement to be in radio contact.

What CBT requires

You must know how to act at traffic lights.

Apart from knowing the sequence of lights, you need to know

- what the colours mean
- how to approach green lights safely
- how to cope with filter lanes
- what to do if traffic lights fail.

You'll also need to know about school crossing warning lights.

Skills you'll acquire

You must be able to

- approach traffic lights at the correct speed
- react to the road and weather conditions
- react correctly to changing lights.

Faults to avoid

- failing to stop at a red light
- approaching green traffic lights too fast
- proceeding into the junction when the green light shows but the way isn't clear
- hesitating as the green light changes and stopping unsafely.

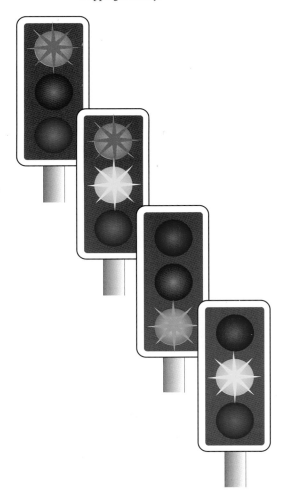

What CBT requires

There are set procedures for dealing with roundabouts.

Your instructor should discuss and demonstrate how to go

- left
- ahead
- right.

This will involve learning how to apply the OSM/PSL routine for the direction you intend to travel. This will include

- signalling procedures
- lane discipline
- observation.

Your instructor will want to see you use safely the correct procedures for each roundabout you deal with.

Skills you'll acquire

You must be able to

- take effective rear observation
- approach at the correct speed
- give the correct signals at the right time
- follow the correct road position throughout
- judge the speed of other traffic
- cancel signals correctly.

Faults to avoid

- giving wrong or misleading signals
- approaching at the wrong speed
- stopping when the way is clear
- positioning incorrectly
- riding out into the path of approaching traffic
- failing to take effective observation.

What CBT requires

You'll have practised turning left and right in Element C. You'll now have to combine those riding skills with real traffic situations.

Your instructor will want to see you deal with a variety of junctions. These may include

- crossroads
- T-junctions
- staggered junctions
- Y-junctions.

You'll be expected to react to signs such as

- warning signs
- 'Stop' signs
- direction signs
- 'No entry' signs
- priority signs

and road markings.

You must show you're aware of other road users and watch for vehicles approaching, emerging or turning.

Skills you'll acquire

To deal safely with junctions you must

- use the OSM/PSL routine correctly as you approach a junction
- position yourself correctly on the road
- control your speed to suit the road, weather and traffic conditions
- obey road signs and markings
- react correctly to other road users
- demonstrate effective observation.

Faults to avoid

All junctions must be treated with great care. Avoid

- stopping or waiting unnecessarily
- approaching a junction too fast
- overtaking as you approach a junction
- riding into a junction unsafely
- incorrect use of signals
- incorrect road position.

The road surface at junctions is often an additional hazard for motorcyclists. If you're riding on a shiny surface don't

- brake fiercely
- accelerate harshly.

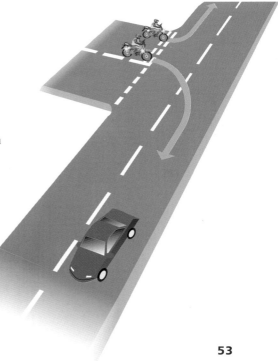

What CBT requires

There's a variety of pedestrian crossings you may encounter:

- zebra
- pelican
- toucan
- puffin.

Your instructor will want to see you

- at a zebra crossing
  - slow down and be prepared to stop for waiting pedestrians
- at pelican, puffin and toucan crossings
  - stop if the red light shows
  - give way to pedestrians on a pelican crossing when the amber lights are flashing
  - give way to cyclists on a toucan crossing, as you would to pedestrians.

Skills you'll acquire

As you approach a pedestrian crossing you need to

- control your speed
- react correctly to pedestrians waiting to cross
- know how and why you would give an arm signal as you stop at a zebra crossing.

Faults to avoid

- approaching a crossing too fast
- failing to stop or show awareness of waiting pedestrians
- stopping across a crossing so blocking the way for pedestrians
- overtaking within the zigzag lines leading up to a crossing
- waving pedestrians across the road
- failing to respond correctly to traffic light signals at controlled crossings.

What CBT requires

During this element your instructor will want to see that you can cope with gradients.

This will entail

- hill start procedures
- riding uphill
- riding downhill.

You should have some understanding of how riding uphill or downhill can affect control of your motorcycle.

Skills you'll acquire

To move off on an uphill gradient you need to have good control of the

- clutch
- throttle.

When riding down a steep hill you need to know how to control your speed using the

- brakes
- gears.

When riding up a steep hill you need to be able to match the gear to the speed and load on the engine.

Faults to avoid

- moving off into the path of passing traffic
- stalling the engine
- rolling backwards.

Element
E

What CBT requires

Any bend can be a hazard. You must be able to recognise the hazard and safely deal with it.

Your instructor will want to see that you

- ride at a speed such that you can stop within the distance you can see
- keep to the correct road position
- are aware of road surface hazards such as
  - drain covers
  - loose surfaces
  - adverse camber.

On left hand bends you will have less view ahead. Be prepared for

- pedestrians
- stopped or broken down vehicles
- cyclists
- stopped vehicles waiting to turn right.

You should know how the weather affects your safety when cornering.

Skills you'll acquire

To help you assess any bend you should be looking out for

- road signs
- road markings
- chevrons.

Approaching a bend you need to

- control your speed
- select the correct gear
- leave a safe gap between you and other vehicles.

You must be able to lean into a bend while steering a steady course.

Faults to avoid

- coasting
- braking while leaning over
- cornering too fast
- leaning over too far
- riding in the wrong position
  - too close to oncoming traffic
  - too close to the gutter.

DSA **CBT AND THE TEST**

What CBT requires

Obstructions are another hazard you will need to deal with.

To deal safely with these your instructor will want to see that you're riding defensively.

That's always riding

- at the correct speed for the road, weather and traffic conditions
- in the correct position
- in the correct gear
- looking ahead, anticipating and preparing for changing situations.

Skills you'll acquire

How well you cope with an obstruction depends largely on how well you plan ahead. To cope with hazards you need to be

- looking well ahead
- giving yourself time and space to react
- using the OSM/PSL routine
- in the correct position
- in full control of your speed.

Your attitude can affect how easily you learn these skills.

Faults to avoid

- failing to look far enough ahead
- reacting too late
- riding too fast
- approaching an obstruction in the wrong gear.

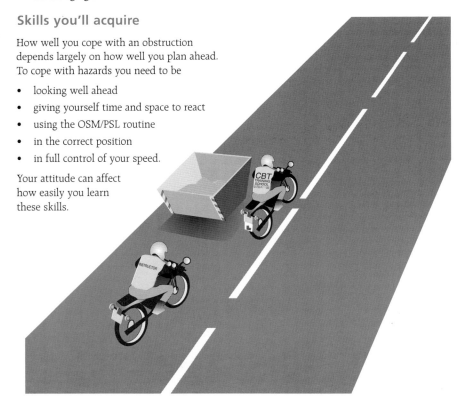

What CBT requires

As part of Element C you practised riding a U-turn on the training area.

During this element you'll be expected to ride a U-turn on the road.

This

- builds on the skills you learned earlier
- helps prepare you for your practical motorcycle test.

Your instructor will find a quiet side road and explain what's required.

You cannot complete Element E until your instructor is satisfied you can safely ride a U-turn on the road.

Skills you'll acquire

You'll need the machine control skills of

- balance
- steering
- clutch/throttle.

You'll have to develop these skills to include coping with

- the camber of the road
- the possibility of passing traffic
- kerbs on either side.

Faults to avoid

- failure to take effective observation before or during the exercise
- riding into the kerb or onto the pavement
- using your feet to help balance
- harsh, clumsy use of the clutch and throttle.

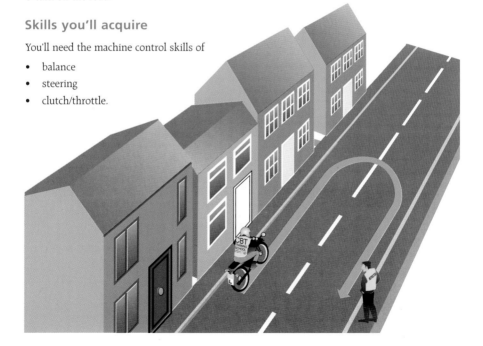

What CBT requires

You've learnt and practised this exercise in Element C.

In this element you repeat the exercise but in an on-road situation. This will

- develop your earlier skills
- help ensure your safety if an emergency does arise
- prepare you for performing this exercise on your practical motorcycle test.

Your instructor will find a quiet side road and explain the signal to be used.

You'll then be expected to ride at normal speed before being given the signal to stop.

At no time will your instructor let you ride off out of sight.

Skills you'll acquire

- quick reaction to the 'stop' signal
- use of both brakes in the appropriate ratio
- the ability to quickly correct a locked wheel.

Faults to avoid

- riding too slowly before the signal
- taking rear observation before reacting to the stop signal
- locking one or both wheels and failing to correct the fault
- stopping too slowly
- moving off unsafely after stopping.

The topics covered

- After CBT
- The theory test
- About the practical test
- How to apply for your practical test
- Attending your practical test.

After CBT

CBT will give you the foundations on which to build a safe motorcycling career. Like all new skills you need

- training
- practice

to become good at them.

Training

Many ATBs provide additional training up to practical test standard. When you attend for this training you may find you are in a group with other learners. There is maximum ratio of four learners to each instructor for post CBT training using learner machines.

Sometimes ATBs can book your practical test appointment at the local driving test centre.

Ask your instructor about further training and make sure the full syllabus is covered (see Part six).

Practise

- on as many different types of road as you can
- on dual carriageways where the national speed limit applies
- in all sorts of traffic conditions – even in the dark.

You'll be asked to ride on a variety of road types during the test. Don't just concentrate on

- roads near the test centre
- the exercises included in the test.

When you practise try not to

- obstruct other traffic. Most drivers are tolerant of learners, but don't try their patience too much
- annoy local residents. For example, by practising emergency stops in quiet residential streets.

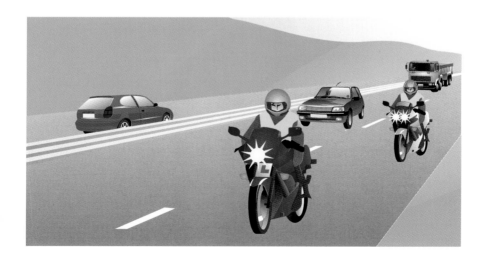

The theory test

The theory test will gauge your knowledge and understanding of riding theory. A sound knowledge of the theory is essential to a better understanding of practical riding skills.

Theory test sessions are available during weekdays, evenings and on Saturdays. A test appointment will normally be available for you within about two weeks.

There are theory test centres throughout Great Britain and Northern Ireland. You can find out where your local centre is from

- your ATB
- a DSA driving test centre
- the telephone information line 0870 01 01 372.

Who's affected?

All motorcycle test candidates will have to pass the theory test before a booking for a practical test will be accepted.*

Ready for your test?

Make sure that you're well prepared before you attempt the test. Study your copy of *The Highway Code* and the publication *The Official Theory Test for Motorcyclists* (both published by The Stationery Office).

It's very important that you know why the answers are correct. Take this knowledge and put it into practice on the road. Your examiner will expect you to demonstrate what you have learned through your riding.

*Note

You will not have to take a theory test if you hold a full moped licence obtained by passing both a theory and practical moped test.

Booking a theory test

Some ATBs will be able to book your theory test for you. Alternatively you can book your test by telephone or by post.

Booking by telephone You can use your credit or debit card. The person who books the test must be the card holder.

If you book by this method you'll be given the date and time of your test immediately. You can do this by calling **0870 01 01 372** or **0845 600 6700** for Northern Ireland at any time between 8 am and 6 pm Monday to Friday. When you phone you should have ready your

- driving licence number
- credit or debit card details.

If you are deaf and need a minicom machine telephone **0870 01 06 372.**

Welsh speakers can telephone **0870 01 00 372.**

You'll be given a booking number and sent an appointment letter that you should expect to receive within four days of your call. If not contact the booking office to check that the appointment was made.

Booking by post Application forms are available from

- theory test centres
- driving test centres
- your ATB.

You should receive an appointment letter within 10 days of posting your application form. If not, telephone the booking office to check that your application was received and that a test appointment has been made.

Special needs

If you have special needs please state this on your application form. Every effort will be made to ensure that the appropriate arrangements are made for you.

Cancelling a theory test

To cancel or postpone a theory test appointment you should contact the booking office at least three clear working days before the test date, otherwise you will lose your fee. Only in exceptional circumstances like documented ill-health or family bereavement can this rule be waived.

Attending

When you attend your theory test you'll have to show photographic evidence of your identity as well as your driving licence. See page 69 for details of acceptable forms of photographic identity.

Arrive in plenty of time so that you aren't rushed. The test centre staff will check your documents and ensure that you receive the right category test. If you arrive after the session has started you may not be allowed to sit the test.

If you pass

The result should be available at the centre within 30 minutes of completing your test. If you've passed you'll be issued with a pass certificate. Take this with you when you attend your practical test.

The pass certificate will be valid for two years. You must take and pass the practical test within that time or you'll have to take the theory test again.

If you fail

If you haven't passed the theory test then you must retake it. You'll have to wait a minimum of three clear working days before you take the test again.

About the practical test

You will pass if you can show your examiner that you can

- ride safely
- complete the special exercises
- demonstrate through your riding that you have a thorough knowledge of *The Highway Code.*

What's the purpose of the test?

The practical test is designed to gauge whether you can ride safely. The test ensures that all riders reach a minimum standard.

How long will the test last?

About 40 minutes.

What will the test include?

Apart from general riding, your test will include

- an eyesight test
- special exercises, such as an emergency stop.

What's the order of the test?

The eyesight test is first. If your eyesight isn't up to the standard the test won't continue. After the eyesight test the order is up to the examiner.

How will the examiner test me?

Before the test you will be fitted with

- earphones under your helmet
- a radio receiver on a waist belt.

When you're taking the test your examiner will follow you either on a motorcycle or in a car. Before the emergency stop exercise your examiner will stand next to you and give you your instructions.

Your test will be carried out over a route covering a wide variety of road and traffic conditions.

At the end of the test your examiner will ask you a question about carrying a pillion passengers on your machine.

Throughout the test you should demonstrate the knowledge you have gained from studying for your theory test.

What about the special exercises?

The first special exercise is usually the emergency stop. This normally comes after a short ride. The examiner will be as helpful as possible and will

- ask you to pull up on the left
- explain any one of the special exercises and ask you to carry it out.

Make sure that you understand. If you aren't sure about anything, ask! The examiner will explain again.

You'll be required to demonstrate the other special exercises while riding over the test route.

What will the examiner expect?

The examiner will want to see that you ride safely and competently under various road and traffic conditions.

You'll be

- given directions clearly and in good time
- asked to carry out special exercises.

The examiner will be understanding and sympathetic and will make every effort to put you at ease.

How will I know when I'm ready for the practical test?

If you have taken additional training, be guided by your instructor, who has the knowledge and experience to tell you when you're ready.

You must be able to ride

- consistently well and with confidence
- without assistance and guidance from your instructor.

If you can't, you aren't ready for the test. Waiting until you are ready will save you time and money.

How should I ride during the test?

The examiner will be looking for an overall safe ride. If you make a mistake, don't worry. It might not affect the result.

Does the standard of the test vary?

No. All examiners are trained to carry out tests to the same standard.

Test routes

- are as uniform as possible
- include a range of typical road and traffic conditions.

Are examiners supervised?

Examiners are frequently supervised by a senior officer. If a senior officer is present at your test, don't worry.

The senior officer

- checks that the examiner is testing you properly
- won't interfere with the test or the result.

Passing the test

You'll pass if you can satisfy the examiner that you can

- ride safely
- comply with correct road procedure
- obey traffic signs
- carry out the special exercises correctly.

When you've passed

You'll be allowed to ride

- without L-plates
- unsupervised
- on motorways.

The size of motorcycle you'll be licensed to ride immediately after passing your test will depend on the machine you've used to take the test. See page 70.

How your practical test is assessed

Your examiner will assess any errors you make and, depending on their degree of seriousness, record them on the Driving Test Report form (DL25). You will fail your test if you commit a serious or dangerous fault. You will also fail if you commit more than a fixed number of driving faults.

The criteria the examiner will use are as follows

Driving fault – less serious, but has been assessed as such because of circumstances at that particular time. An accumulation of more than a fixed number of driving faults will result in a fail.

Serious fault – recorded when a potentially dangerous incident has occurred or a habitual driving fault indicates a serious weakness in a your riding.

Dangerous fault – recorded when a fault is assessed as having caused actual danger during the test.

At the end of the test you will be offered some general guidance to explain your Driving Test Report.

Explanatory Markings

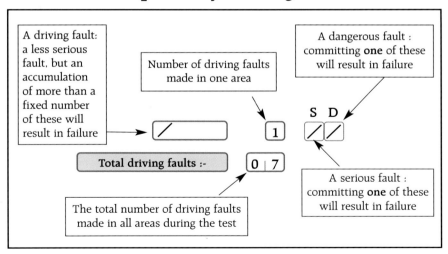

How to apply for your practical test

You can apply for a practical test by

- post
- telephone.

By post Fill out an application form, DL 26, which is available from any DSA driving test centre.

Full details of fees can be obtained from any driving test centre or DSA Enquiries and Booking Centre; telephone 0870 01 01 372.

Complete the form and send it with the appropriate fee to the address given.

If you wish to take your test in Wales using the Welsh language, please indicate this on the form.

By phone Call the DSA Enquiries and Booking Centre; telephone 0870 01 01 372. Minicom users should telephone 0870 01 07 372 and Welsh speakers 0870 01 00 372. DSA accepts most major credit and debit cards.

Apply well before you want to be tested and give the earliest date you think you'll be ready.

Trainer booking

Your training organisation may be able to provide you with a test appointment. Make sure you provide all the information they ask you for, or the booking may be delayed.

Your test appointment

DSA will send you an appointment card. This will give you

- the time and date of the appointment
- the address of the driving test centre
- other important information.

You should normally receive notification within two weeks of your application. If you don't, contact the DSA Enquiries and Booking Centre, without delay.

Postponing your test appointment

Contact DSA if

- the date or time on the card isn't suitable
- you want to postpone or cancel the test

You must give at least ten clear working days' notice (that is, two weeks – longer if there's a bank holiday) not counting

- the day DSA received your request
- the day of the test.

If you don't give enough notice you'll lose your fee.

Saturday and evening tests

Tests are available at some driving test centres on Saturdays and weekday evenings. These test times have a higher fee.

Attending your practical test

Make sure that you bring with you

- your appointment card
- your driving licence and make sure that you've signed it. If you have a photocard licence you must bring with you the counterpart which is part of the licence
- your theory test pass certificate
- photographic evidence of your identity (if not presenting a photocard licence)
- your CBT certificate. Your examiner will ask to see it. If you cannot show your CBT certificate or it has expired your test will not be conducted.

You'll also have to sign a declaration that your machine is insured. If you can't comply with any of these requirements the examiner may not be able to conduct the test.

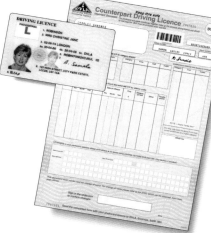

Photographic identity

If your licence does not show your photograph you must also bring with you a form of photographic identification. For this your examiner will accept

- a signed passport or document of like nature. The passport does not have to be a British one
- any of the following identification cards, provided it has your photograph and your signature
  - workplace identity card
  - trade union or students' union membership card
  - card for the purchase of rail tickets
  - school bus pass
  - cheque guarantee card or credit card
  - gun licence
  - proof of age card (issued by the Portman Group)
- a photograph of yourself, which has been signed and dated on the back by an acceptable person, confirming that the photograph is a true likeness of you. A signature will be accepted from the following
  - Approved Driving Instructor
  - DSA certified motorcycle instructor
  - Member of Parliament
  - local authority councillor
  - teacher (qualified)
  - Justice of the Peace
  - civil servant (established)
  - police officer
  - bank official
  - minister of religion
  - barrister or solicitor
  - medical practitioner
  - LGV Trainer on DSA Voluntary Register of LGV Instructors
  - commissioned officer in HM Forces.

Your test will be cancelled if you can't provide one of these forms of identification.

I_____(name of certifier), certify that this is a true likeness of_____, who has been known to me for (number) months / years in my capacity as
_____
Signed _____
Dated _____
Daytime phone no._____
ADI/CBT Instructor no._____

Your test motorcycle

Make sure that the motorcycle you intend to ride during your test is

- legally roadworthy and has a current test certificate, if it's over the prescribed age
- fully covered by insurance for you to ride and for its present use
- of the correct engine size/power output for the category of test that you're taking
- properly licensed with the correct tax disc displayed
- displaying L-plates (or D-plates in Wales) which are visible from the front and rear.

If you overlook any of these your test may be cancelled and you could lose your fee.

Test motorcycle to obtain a light motorcycle licence

Test motorcycle to obtain a standard motorcycle licence

Test motorcycles

- Motorcycles less than 75 cc aren't acceptable for the practical motorcycle test.
- Only the disabled can use a motorcycle and sidecar combination for the test. The licence obtained will be restricted to such combinations.
- If you pass your test on a motorcycle with automatic or semi-automatic transmission this will be recorded on your licence. Your full licence entitlement will be restricted to motorcycles in this category.

Test motorcycle for Direct and Accelerated access

Disabilities or special circumstances

To make sure that enough time is allowed for your test, it would help DSA to know if you

- are deaf or have severe hearing difficulties
- are in any way restricted in your movements
- have any disability which may affect your riding.

If any one of these apply to you, please write this on your application form or inform the booking clerk when making a telephone booking.

If you can't speak English or are deaf, you're allowed to bring an interpreter (who must not be your instructor). The interpreter must be at least 16 years of age.

PART FOUR THE MOTORCYCLE TEST

This part looks at what the test requires.

The topics covered

- The eyesight test
- Theory into practice
- Before you start the engine
- The motorcycle controls
- Moving off
- Rear observation
- Giving signals
- Acting on signs and signals
- Controlling your speed
- Making progress
- The emergency stop
- Special exercises
- Hazards
- Selecting a safe place to stop
- Awareness and anticipation.

What the test requires

You must satisfy your examiner that, in good daylight, you can read a vehicle number plate with letters 79.4 mm (3.1 in.) high at a **minimum distance** of 20.5 metres (about 67 feet).

When number plates with the narrower font are introduced the minimum distance will be 20 m (about 66 feet).

If you need glasses or contact lenses to read the number plate, that is fine. However, you must wear them during the test and whenever you ride.

If you have had sight correction surgery you should declare this when you apply for your provisional licence.

How your examiner will test you

Before you begin riding, your examiner will point out a vehicle and ask you to read its number plate.

If you can't speak English or have difficulty reading, you may copy down what you see.

If your answer is incorrect, your examiner will measure the exact distance and repeat the test.

If you fail the eyesight test

If you can't show your examiner that your eyesight is up to the required standard

- you will have failed your motorcycle test
- your test will go no further.

If you normally wear glasses or contact lenses, always wear them whenever you ride.

What the test requires

You must satisfy your examiner that you have **fully understood** everything which you learned for the theory test.

The aspects are

- alertness and concentration
- courtesy and consideration
- care in the use of the controls to reduce mechanical wear and tear
- awareness of stopping distances and safety margins in all conditions
- hazard awareness
- correct action concerning pedestrians and other vulnerable road users
- dealing with other types of vehicle in the correct manner
- rules regarding speed limits and stopping restrictions
- road and traffic signs.

You will also be expected to know

- the law regarding you and your vehicle
- what to do in the event of an accident
- the effect extra loads have on your vehicle
- the effect motoring has on the environment.

What your examiner wants to see

Before you start the engine you must always check that

- the fuel tap is turned on
- the engine kill switch is in the 'on' position
- the gear lever is in neutral.

Faults to avoid

You shouldn't

- use the fuel tap's reserve position instead of the 'on' position. The motorcycle will run normally but you'll have no warning when your fuel is running low.
- use the clutch to allow you to start the engine without first having found neutral.

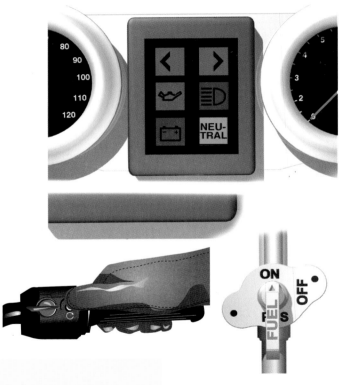

Note

Many road safety organisations recommend the use of dipped headlights at all times.

BE SEEN BE SAFE

What the test requires

You should show your examiner that you understand the functions of all the controls.

You should use them

- smoothly
- correctly
- safely
- at the right time.

The main controls are

- throttle
- clutch
- front brake
- rear brake
- steering
- gears.

You should

- understand what these controls do
- be able to use them competently.

If you are riding an automatic motorcycle

Make sure that you fully understand the controls before you attempt to ride a motorcycle with automatic transmission.

Throttle and clutch

Skills you should show

You should

- balance the throttle and clutch to pull away smoothly
- accelerate gradually to gain speed
- pull the clutch in just before the motorcycle stops.

If you're riding a motorcycle with automatic or semi-automatic transmission, you should

- ensure that the brakes are used to prevent creeping forward
- control the throttle when
  - moving off
  - changing gear.

Faults to avoid

You shouldn't

- accelerate fiercely. This can lead to a loss of control and may distract or alarm other road users
- use the clutch in a jerky and uncontrolled manner when moving off or changing gear.

Brakes and gears

Skills you should show

Brakes You should

- use both brakes correctly and in good time
- brake lightly in most situations.

Gears You should

- choose the right gear for your speed and the road conditions
- change gear in good time so that you are ready for a hazard or junction.

Faults to avoid

Brakes You shouldn't

- brake harshly, except in an emergency.
- use either the front or rear brake alone.

Gears You shouldn't

- select the wrong gear
- coast with the clutch lever pulled in or the gear lever in neutral.

Steering

Skills you should show

You should

- keep both hands on the handlebars
- keep your steering movements steady and smooth
- begin turning at the correct time when turning a corner
- show awareness of the road surface.

Faults to avoid

Don't turn too early when steering around a corner. If you do, you risk

- cutting the corner when turning right and putting others at risk
- striking the kerb when turning left.

Don't turn too late. You could put other road users at risk by

- swinging wide on left turns
- overshooting right turns.

You shouldn't

- brake and steer together
- lean the motorcycle over too far and cause one or both tyres to lose their grip
- move out before turning left.

DSA CBT AND THE TEST

What the test requires

You should understand

- the functions of all controls and switches which have a bearing on road safety such as
  - indicators
  - horn
  - lights.

  You should know where to find these controls on the motorcycle you are riding

- the meaning of gauges or other instruments including
  - speedometer
  - various warning lights.

Safety checks

You should also be able to carry out routine safety checks such as

- oil and coolant levels
- tyre pressures
- the use of the emergency stop switch
- correct drive chain adjustment.

In addition, you should be able to identify defects, especially with

- steering
- brakes
- tyres
- lights
- reflectors
- horn
- speedometer
- exhaust system
- direction indicators.

You should understand the effects which extra loads such as

- luggage
- a pillion passenger

have on your motorcycle.

What the test requires

You should be able to move off

- safely
- under control
- on the flat
- from behind a parked car
- on a hill, where appropriate.

How your examiner will test you

Your examiner will watch your

- use of the controls each time you move off
- observation of other road users.

Skills you should show

Use your mirrors and signal if necessary.

Before you move off, look around over your shoulder and check any blind spots that can't be seen in your mirror. Check for

- traffic
- pedestrians.

Move off under control making balanced use of the

- throttle
- clutch
- brakes
- steering.

You should also ensure that you move off in the correct gear.

Faults to avoid

You shouldn't

- immediately signal without first taking effective observation around you
- pull out without looking
- cause other road users to stop or alter their course
- accelerate excessively
- move off in too high a gear
- fail to coordinate the controls correctly and stall the engine.

What the test requires

Make sure that you take effective rear observation

- before any manoeuvre
- to keep aware of what is happening behind you.

Check carefully before

- moving off
- signalling
- changing direction
- turning to the left or right
- overtaking or changing lanes
- increasing speed
- slowing down or stopping.

How your examiner will test you

Your examiner will watch your use of rear observation as you ride.

Skills you should show

Use the Observation – Signal – Manoeuvre (OSM) routine.

You should

- look before you signal
- look and signal before you act
- act sensibly and safely on what you see when you have taken rear observation.

You should be aware that the mirrors won't show everything behind you.

Faults to avoid

You shouldn't

- manoeuvre without taking rear observation
- fail to act on what you see behind.

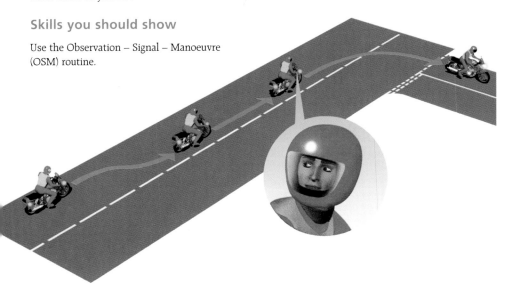

What the test requires

You should signal

- to let others know what you intend to do
- to help other road users, including pedestrians
- in plenty of time.

You must only use the signals shown in *The Highway Code.*

Your signals should help other road users

- to understand what you intend to do
- to react safely.

Always make sure that your signal is cancelled after use.

How your examiner will test you

Your examiner will watch carefully how you use your signals as you ride.

Skills you should show

Give signals

- clearly
- in good time.

You should also know how to give arm signals and when they are necessary.

Faults to avoid

You shouldn't

- give signals carelessly
- mislead other road users
- forget to cancel the signal
- wave at pedestrians to cross the road.

What the test requires

You should be able to understand

- all traffic signs
- all road markings.

React to them in good time.

At the beginning of the test your examiner will ask you to follow the road ahead.

You will be **asked** to turn at junctions, but look out for lane markings and direction signs. You will be expected to act on these.

Traffic lights

You must act correctly at traffic lights.

When the green light shows, check that the road is clear before proceeding.

Signals by authorised persons

You must obey the signals given by

- police officers
- traffic wardens
- school crossing patrols.

Traffic calming measures

Take extra care on roads which have been altered by the addition of

- 20 mph speed limit zones
- speed restriction humps
- width restrictions marked by bollards, posts or paved areas.

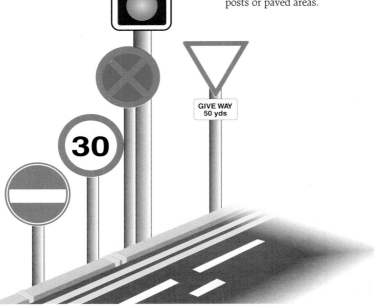

What the test requires

You should make good progress along the road bearing in mind

- road conditions
- traffic
- weather
- road signs and speed limits.

How your examiner will test you

Your examiner will watch carefully your control of speed as you ride.

Skills you should show

You should

- take great care in the use of speed
- make sure that you can stop safely, well within the distance you can see to be clear
- leave a safe distance between yourself and other vehicles
- leave extra distance on wet or slippery roads
- approach junctions and hazards at the correct speed.

Faults to avoid

You shouldn't

- ride too fast for the road and traffic conditions
- change your speed unpredictably.

What the test requires

You should

- make reasonable progress along the road
- ride at a speed appropriate to road and traffic conditions
- move off at junctions as soon as it's safe to do so.

How your examiner will test you

Your examiner will watch your riding and will want to see you

- make reasonable progress along the road
- keep up with traffic
- show confidence, together with sound judgement
- comply with the speed limits.

Skills you should show

You should be able to choose the correct speed for the

- type of road
- road surface
- type and density of traffic
- weather and visibility.

You should approach all hazards at a safe speed.

Faults to avoid

You shouldn't

- ride too slowly, holding up other traffic
- be over-cautious or stop and wait when it's safe to go
- prepare too early for junctions by approaching too slowly and holding up traffic.

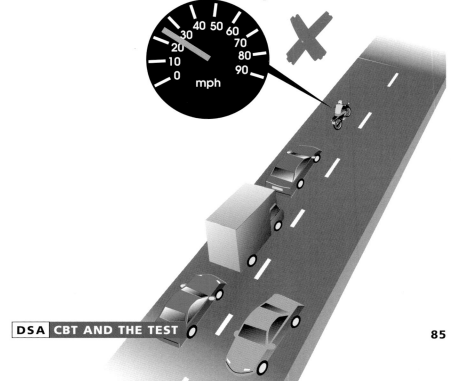

What the test requires

In an emergency you should be able to stop the motorcycle

- as quickly as possible
- safely and under control
- without locking the wheels.

How your examiner will test you

Your examiner will

- ask you to pull up on the side of the road
- explain the procedure
- demonstrate the signal to you.

When your examiner gives the signal, try to stop the motorcycle as you would in a real emergency:

- you should react quickly
- try to stop in a straight line
- take special care if the road is wet.

Your examiner will check that the road is clear behind you before the signal is given.

Skills you should show

You should stop the motorcycle

- in a short distance
- under full control
- without risk to other road users.

Faults to avoid

You shouldn't

- anticipate the signal by slowing or stopping while your examiner is checking the road behind
- skid out of control
- pull up slowly.

Walking with your machine

Your examiner will ask you to put your machine on its stand. You will then be asked to take the machine off its stand and to walk with it, normally in a U-turn, but without the aid of the engine.

Riding a U-turn

Your examiner will ask you to ride a U-turn. Direct rear observation into the blind area is vital just before you carry out the manoeuvre.

Angle start

Your examiner will ask you to pull up just before a parked vehicle. Before you move off, make sure that you check

- to the rear and into the blind area
- ahead to see there is no danger from approaching traffic.

If an angle start occurs normally during the test, you may not be asked to do it again.

Slow ride

You will be asked to ride along at a walking speed for a short distance.

This exercise tests your control, balance and observation. If you have already ridden slowly, such as in traffic, you may not be asked to carry out this exercise.

Hill start

Your examiner might ask you to pull up on an uphill gradient.

When moving off, your machine could be slower accelerating. You will need to remember this when judging the moment to ride off.

What is a hazard?

A hazard is any situation which could involve adjusting speed or altering course.

Look well ahead where there are

- road junctions or roundabouts
- parked vehicles
- cyclists or horse riders
- pedestrian crossings.

By identifying the hazard early you will have time to take the appropriate action.

You may have to deal with several hazards at once or during a short space of time. This may mean using your initiative and common sense to deal with the particular circumstances.

What the test requires

Observation – Signal –Manoeuvre (OSM/PSL routine)

Always use this routine when approaching a hazard.

- **O**bservation
- **S**ignal
- **M**anoeuvre.

Observation   Check the position of following traffic using your mirrors or by looking behind at an appropriate time.

Signal   If necessary, signal your intention to change course or slow down. Signal clearly and in good time.

Manoeuvre   A manoeuvre is any change of speed or position, from slowing or stopping to turning off a busy road. Manoeuvre has three phases:

- **P**osition
- **S**peed
- **L**ook.

You should consider each phase in turn and use them as appropriate.

What the test requires

You should

- use the OSM routine when you approach a junction or a roundabout
- position your motorcycle correctly. Adjust your speed and stop if necessary
- use the correct lane if the road has lane markings. In a one-way street choose that lane as soon as you can do so safely.

If the road has no lane markings, when turning left, keep to the left.

Watch out for

- cyclists
- pedestrians crossing.

When turning right, you should

- keep as close to the centre of the road as is safe
- use effective observation before you enter a junction
- make a 'lifesaver' check over your right shoulder before you turn.

How your examiner will test you

Your examiner will watch carefully and take account of your

- use of the OSM/PSL routine
- position and speed on approach
- observation and judgement.

Skills you should show

You should be able to

- observe road signs and markings and act correctly on what you see
- judge the correct speed on approach
- slow down in good time, without harsh braking
- judge the speed of the other traffic, especially at roundabouts and when you are joining major roads
- position and turn correctly.

Faults to avoid

You shouldn't

- approach the junction at the wrong speed
- position and turn incorrectly
- enter a junction unsafely
- stop or wait unnecessarily.

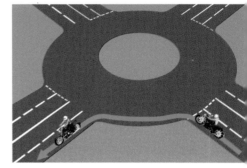

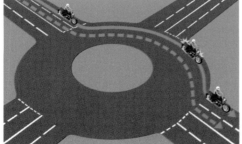

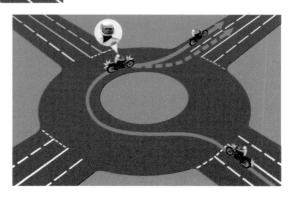

What the test requires

When overtaking you must

- observe any signs and road markings which prohibit overtaking
- allow enough room
- give cyclists and horses at least as much room as a car. They might swerve or wobble suddenly
- allow enough space after overtaking. Don't cut in.

How your examiner will test you

Your examiner will watch and take into account how you

- use the OSM/PSL routine
- react to road and traffic conditions
- handle the controls.

Skills you should show

You should be able to judge the speed and position of vehicles

- behind, which might be trying to overtake you
- in front, if you are planning to overtake
- coming towards you.

Overtake only when you can do so

- safely
- without causing other vehicles to slow down or alter course.

Faults to avoid

You shouldn't overtake when

- your view of the road ahead isn't clear
- you would have to exceed the speed limit
- there is oncoming traffic and you are squeezing between the oncoming traffic and the vehicle you are overtaking
- the road is narrow.

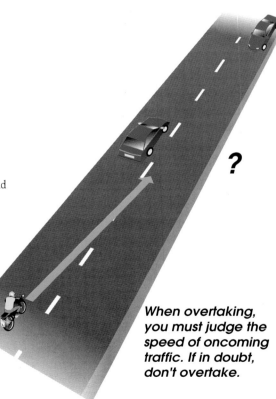

When overtaking, you must judge the speed of oncoming traffic. If in doubt, don't overtake.

What the test requires

You should deal with oncoming traffic safely and confidently. This applies

- on narrow roads
- where there are parked cars or other obstructions.

If there is an obstruction on your side of the road, or not enough space for two vehicles to pass safely, you should

- use the OSM/PSL routine
- be prepared to give way to oncoming traffic.

If you need to stop, keep well back from the obstruction to give yourself

- a better view of the road ahead
- room to move off easily when the road is clear.

When you are passing parked cars, allow at least the width of a car door, if possible.

How your examiner will test you

Your examiner will watch carefully and take into account how you

- use the OSM/PSL routine
- react to road and traffic conditions
- handle the controls.

Skills you should show

You should

- show judgement and control when meeting oncoming traffic
- be decisive when stopping and moving off
- allow enough room when passing parked cars.

Watch out for

- doors opening
- children running out into the road
- pedestrians stepping out from the pavement
- vehicles pulling out without warning.

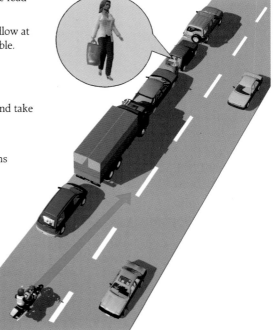

What the test requires

You should be able to cross the path of oncoming vehicles safely and with confidence.

You normally need to cross the path of other vehicles when you have to turn right into a side road or driveway. You should

- use the OSM/PSL routine
- position correctly and adjust your speed
- watch out for oncoming traffic and stop if necessary.

Watch out for pedestrians

- crossing the side road
- on the pavement, if you are entering a driveway.

How your examiner will test you

Your examiner will watch carefully and take account of your judgement of the oncoming traffic.

Skills you should show

You should show that you can turn right into a junction or driveway safely, using the OSM/PSL routine.

Faults to avoid

You shouldn't cause oncoming vehicles to

- slow down
- swerve
- stop.

You shouldn't

- cut the corner
- go beyond the correct turning point before you begin to turn.

What the test requires

You should always ride so that you can stop in the distance you can see to be clear.

Always keep a safe distance between yourself and the vehicle in front.

In good conditions, leave a gap of at least one metre (just over three feet) for every mile per hour you are travelling. Or leave a two-second time gap.

In bad conditions, leave at least double the distance, or a four-second time gap.

In slow-moving, congested traffic it may not be practical to leave so much space.

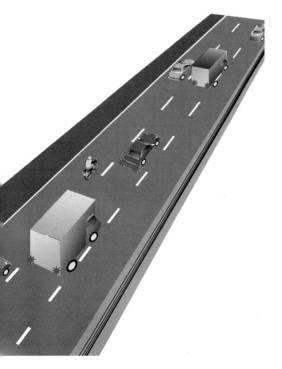

How your examiner will test you

Your examiner will watch carefully and take account of how you

- use the OSM/PSL routine
- anticipate situations
- react to changing road and traffic conditions
- handle the controls.

Skills you should show

You should

- be able to judge a safe separation distance between you and the vehicle in front
- show correct use of the OSM/PSL routine, especially before reducing speed
- avoid the need to brake harshly if the vehicle in front slows down or stops
- take extra care when your view ahead is limited by large vehicles such as lorries or buses.

Watch out for

- brake lights ahead
- direction indicators
- vehicles ahead braking without warning.

Faults to avoid

You shouldn't

- follow too closely
- brake suddenly
- stop too close to the vehicle in front in a traffic queue.

What the test requires

You should

- normally keep well to the left
- keep clear of parked vehicles
- avoid weaving in and out between parked vehicles
- position your vehicle correctly for the direction you intend to take.

You should obey all lane markings, especially

- bus and cycle lanes
- in one-way streets

and be particularly aware of left- or right-turn arrows at junctions.

How your examiner will test you

Your examiner will watch carefully to see that you

- use the OSM/PSL routine
- select the correct lane in good time.

Skills you should show

You should

- plan ahead and choose the correct lane in good time
- use the OSM/PSL routine correctly
- position your vehicle sensibly, even if there are no road markings.

Faults to avoid

You shouldn't

- ride too close to the kerb
- ride too close to the centre of the road
- change lanes at the last moment or without good reason
- hinder other road users by being badly positioned or being in the wrong lane
- cut across the path of other traffic in another lane at roundabouts.

What the test requires

You should

- recognise the different types of pedestrian crossing
- show courtesy and consideration towards pedestrians
- stop safely when necessary.

At zebra crossings

You must slow down and stop if there is anyone on the crossing.

You should also

- slow down and be prepared to stop if there is anyone waiting to cross
- know how to give the correct arm signal, if necessary, before slowing down or stopping.

At pelican, puffin and toucan crossings

You must

- stop if the lights are red
- give way to any pedestrians on a pelican crossing when the amber lights are flashing
- give way to cyclists on a toucan crossing, as you would to pedestrians.

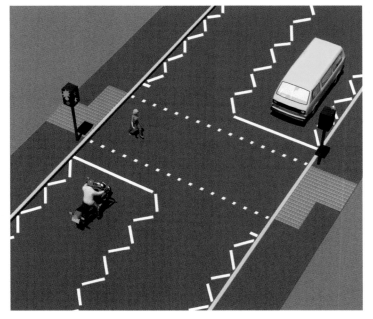

DSA CBT AND THE TEST

How your examiner will test you

Your examiner will watch carefully and take account of how you deal with pedestrian crossings.

Skills you should show

You should be able to

- approach a pedestrian crossing at a controlled speed
- stop safely when necessary
- move off when it's safe, keeping a good lookout.

Faults to avoid

Don't

- approach a crossing too fast
- ride over a crossing without stopping or showing awareness of waiting pedestrians
- block a crossing by stopping directly on it.

Don't hurry pedestrians by

- sounding your horn
- revving your engine
- edging forward.

Don't

- overtake within the zigzag white lines leading up to crossings
- wave pedestrians across
- take late or incorrect action on traffic light signals at controlled crossings.

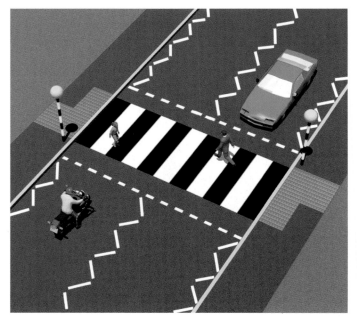

What the test requires

When you make a normal stop you should be able to select a place where you won't

- obstruct the road
- create a hazard.

You should stop close to the edge of the road.

How your examiner will test you

Your examiner will take account of your

- use of the OSM/PSL routine
- judgement in selecting a safe place to stop.

Skills you should show

You should know how and where to stop without causing inconvenience or danger to other road users.

Faults to avoid

You shouldn't

- stop without sufficient warning to other road users
- cause danger or inconvenience to other road users when you stop.

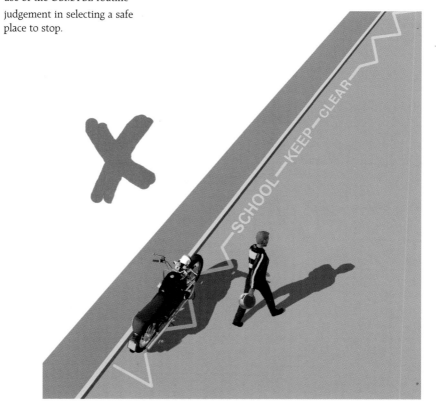

What the test requires

You should be aware of other road users at all times. Also, always plan ahead.

You should

- judge what other road users are likely to do
- predict how their actions will affect you
- react safely and in good time.

Skills you should show

You should show awareness of, and consideration for, all other road users. Anticipation of possible danger and concern for safety should also be shown.

Pedestrians

You should

- give way to pedestrians when turning from one road to another
- take particular care with the very young, the disabled and the elderly. They may not have seen you and could step out suddenly.

Cyclists

Take special care

- when crossing bus or cycle lanes
- with cyclists passing on your left
- with child cyclists.

Animals

Take special care around animals. Give horse riders and other animal handlers as much room as you can. Watch young, possibly inexperienced, riders closely for signs of any difficulty with their mounts. Plan your approach carefully.

Faults to avoid

You shouldn't

- react suddenly to road or traffic conditions
- show irritation with other road users
- sound the horn aggressively
- rev your engine or edge forward when waiting for pedestrians to cross a road.

This part looks at what is required when being tested after disqualification.

The topics covered

- New Drivers Act
- The extended test.

New Drivers Act

Special rules apply for the first two years after the date of passing your practical test if you held nothing but a provisional licence before passing your test.

How you may be affected

Your licence will be revoked if the number of penalty points on your licence reaches six or more as a result of offences you commit before the two years are over. This includes offences you committed before passing your test.

You must then apply for a provisional licence, and from 1 February 2001 complete CBT, before riding on the road. You may ride only as a learner until you pass the theory and practical test again.

This applies even if you pay by fixed penalty.

Endorsements *(as supplied by convicting Court) See leaflet INS 57P for offence codes*

Convicting Court code	Date of conviction			Offence code	Date of offence			Fine £	Disqual. period	Other	Penalty points
	Day	Month	Year		Day	Month	Year				

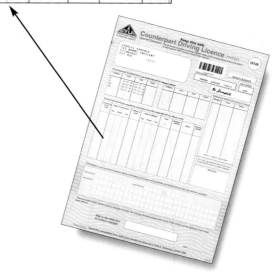

The extended test

Tough penalties exist for anyone convicted of dangerous driving or riding offences.

Courts must

- impose an extended test on anyone convicted of dangerous driving or riding offences.

Courts can also

- impose an extended driving or riding test on anyone convicted of other offences involving obligatory disqualification
- order a normal-length test for other endorsable offences before the disqualified driver or rider can recover a full licence.

Applying for a retest

A rider subject to a retest can apply for a provisional licence at the end of the disqualification period. CBT must be completed before riding on the road.

The normal rules for provisional licence-holders apply:

- L-plates (or, if you wish, D-plates in Wales) must be displayed to the front and rear of the machine
- solo motorcycles must not exceed 125 cc and 11 kW power output (unless riding under the Direct Access Scheme)
- riding on motorways isn't allowed
- pillion passengers may not be carried.

For further information, contact DSA Enquiries and Booking Centre.

The theory test

You will have to pass the theory test before an application for the practical test is accepted.

Details of the theory test can be found in Part Three.

Longer and more demanding

The extended test takes about 70 minutes and covers a wide variety of roads, usually including dual carriageways. This test is more demanding. Make sure that you are ready.

You are advised to take suitable instruction from an approved motorcycle trainer.

Higher fees

The higher fee reflects the longer duration of the test.

How your examiner will test you

Your test will include all the exercises included in the normal test. Your examiner will watch you and take account of

- your ability to concentrate for the duration of the test
- your attitude to other road users.

The topics covered

- If you pass
- If you don't pass
- Officially recommended syllabus
- DSA complaints guide for test candidates
- DSA compensation code for test candidates
- DSA offices and other useful addresses
- Training record

If you pass

Well done! You will have shown that you can ride safely.

You will be given

- a pass certificate (D10, or a D10E in the case of an extended test)
- a copy of the driving test report which will show any riding faults which have been marked during the test
- some general guidance to explain your driving test report.

Look at the report carefully and discuss it with your instructor. It will include notes to help you understand the markings on the form. You may then find it helpful to refer to the relevant sections in this book to help you overcome any weaknesses in your riding.

Remember: under the New Drivers Act your licence could be revoked if you receive six or more penalty points within two years of passing your first test – see page 101.

Developing your riding standards

You should aim to raise your standard of riding with additional instruction and experience.

Ask your instructor about further training including motorway riding.

If you don't pass

Your riding isn't up to the standard required. You made mistakes which could have caused danger on the road.

Your examiner will help you by

- giving you a driving test report form. This will show all the faults marked during the test
- explaining briefly why you haven't passed.

Listen to your examiner carefully. She or he will be able to help you by pointing out the aspects of your riding which you need to improve.

Study the driving test report. It will include notes to help you understand how the examiner marks the form. You may then find it helpful to refer to the relevant sections in this book.

Show your copy of the report to your instructor who will advise and help you to correct the faults. Listen to their advice carefully and get as much practice as you can.

Right of appeal

You will obviously be disappointed if you don't pass your motorcycle test. Although your examiner's decision can't be changed, if you think your test wasn't carried out according to the regulations, you have the right to appeal.

If you live in England and Wales you have six months after the issue of the Statement of Failure in which to appeal (Magistrates' Courts Act 1952 Ch. 55 part VII, Sect. 104).

If you live in Scotland you have 21 days in which to appeal (Sheriff Court, Scotland Act of Sederunt (Statutory Appeals) 1981).

Officially recommended syllabus

Riding is a life skill. It will take you many years to acquire the skills set out here to a high standard.

This syllabus lists the skills in which you must achieve basic competence. You must also have

- a thorough knowledge of *The Highway Code* and motoring laws
- understanding of your responsibilities as a rider.

This means that you must have real concern, not just for your own safety but for the safety of all road users, including pedestrians.

Legal requirements

To learn to ride on the road you must:

1 be aged at least 16 years if you wish to ride a moped, or 17 years if you wish to ride a motorcycle

2 be able to read in good daylight (with glasses or contact lenses, if you wear them) a motor vehicle number plate

- 20.5 metres (about 67 feet) away
- with letters 79.4 mm (3.1 in.) high

When number plates with the narrower font are introduced the minimum distance will be 20 metres (about 66 feet)

3 be medically fit to hold a licence

4 hold a provisional driving licence, or provisional riding entitlement on a full licence for another category

5 comply with the requirements of a provisional licence

- hold a valid Compulsory Basic Training (CBT) certificate

- display L-plates (or, if you wish, D-plates in Wales) to the front and rear of the machine
- pillion passengers must not be carried
- riding on motorways isn't allowed
- solo motorcycles must not exceed 125 cc or 11 kW power output unless learning under the Direct Access Scheme (only open to those over 21 years old), where there are no restrictions to either size or power output

6 ensure that the machine being ridden

- is legally roadworthy
- has a current test certificate if it's over the prescribed age
- displays a valid tax disc
- is covered by appropriate insurance

7 be aware of the legal requirements to notify medical conditions which could affect safe riding. If a machine has been adapted for a disability, ensure that all the adaptations are suitable to control the machine safely

8 wear a safety helmet when riding a motorcycle on road (members of the Sikh religion who wear a turban are exempt)

9 know the rules on the issue, presentation or display of

- driving licences
- insurance certificates
- tax discs.

Rider safety

You must know

1 the safety aspects relating to helmets and how to adjust a helmet correctly

2 the safety factors in wearing suitable clothing and using goggles and visors

Machine controls, equipment and components

You must

1 understand the function of the

- throttle
- clutch
- gears
- front brake
- rear brake
- steering

and be able to adjust (where applicable) and use these competently

2 know the function of all other controls and switches and use them competently

3 understand the meaning of the gauges and other displays on the instrument panel

4 know the legal requirements for the machine

5 be able to carry out routine safety checks such as

- the brakes for correct operation and adjustment
- the steering head for wear and adjustment
- oil and coolant levels
- tyre pressures
- chain tension and condition
- condition of control cables
- suspension
- wheels and tightness of nuts and bolts

and identify defects, especially with the

- steering
- brakes
- tyres

- lights
- reflectors
- direction indicators
- horn
- rear view mirrors
- speedometer
- exhaust system
- chain

6 understand the effects of carrying a load or a pillion passenger will have on the handling of your machine.

Road user behaviour

You must

1 know the most common causes of accidents

2 know which road users are most at risk and how to reduce that risk

3 know the rules, risks and effects of drinking and riding

4 know the effect of fatigue, illness and drugs on riding performance

5 be aware of any age-related problems among other road users, especially among children, teenagers and the elderly

6 be alert and able to anticipate the likely actions of other road users, and be able to take appropriate precautions

7 be aware that courtesy and consideration towards other road users are essential for safe riding.

Machine characteristics

You must

1 know the important principles concerning braking distances and road holding under various road and weather conditions

2 know the handling characteristics of other vehicles with regard to stability, speed, braking and manoeuvrability

3 know that some vehicles are less easily seen than others

4 be able to assess the risks caused by the characteristics of other vehicles and suggest precautions that can be taken, for example:

- large commercial vehicles pulling to the right before turning left
- blind spots for some commercial vehicle drivers
- bicycles and other motorcyclists being buffeted by strong winds.

Road and weather conditions

You must

1 know the particular hazards in both daylight and the dark, and on different types of road, for example

- on single carriageways, including country lanes
- on three-lane roads
- on dual carriageways and motorways

2 gain riding experience on urban and higher-speed roads (but not on motorways) in both daylight and the dark

3 know which road surfaces provide the better or poorer grip when braking

4 know the hazards caused by bad weather, for example:

- rain
- fog
- snow
- ice
- strong winds

5 be able to assess the risks caused by road and traffic conditions, be aware of how the conditions may cause others to drive or ride unsafely, and be able to take appropriate precautions.

Traffic signs, rules and regulations

You must have a sound knowledge of the meaning of traffic signs and road markings, for example

- speed limits
- parking restrictions
- zebra and pelican crossings.

Machine control and road procedure

You must have the knowledge and skills to carry out the following tasks safely and competently, practising the proper use of mirrors, observation and signals:

1 take necessary precautions before mounting or dismounting the machine

2 before starting the engine, carry out safety checks on

* controls
* mirrors

Also check that the gear selector is in neutral

3 start the engine and move off

* straight ahead and at an angle
* on the level, uphill and downhill

4 select the correct road position for normal riding

5 use proper observation in all traffic conditions

6 be able to carry out additional safety checks for two-wheeled vehicles, for example by

* using the mirrors
* looking over the shoulder
* including the 'lifesaver' look

7 be able to use the front and rear brakes correctly

8 know how to lean while turning

9 ride at a speed suitable for road and traffic conditions

10 react promptly to all risks

11 change traffic lanes

12 pass stationary vehicles

13 meet, overtake and cross the path of other vehicles

14 turn right and left at junctions, including crossroads and roundabouts

15 ride ahead at crossroads and roundabouts

16 keep a safe separation distance when following other traffic

17 act correctly at pedestrian crossings

18 show proper regard for the safety of other road users, with particular care towards the most vulnerable

19 ride on both urban and rural roads and, where possible, dual carriageways – keeping up with the flow of traffic where it's safe and proper to do so

20 comply with traffic regulations and traffic signals given by the police, traffic wardens and other road users

21 stop the machine safely, normally and in an emergency, without locking the wheels

22 be able to make a U-turn safely

23 be able to keep the machine balanced at all speeds

24 be able to wheel the machine, without the aid of the engine, by walking alongside it

25 be able to park and remove the machine from its stand

26 cross all types of railway level crossing.

Additional knowledge

You must know

1 the importance of correct tyre pressures

2 the action needed to avoid and correct skids

3 how to ride through floods and flooded areas

4 what to do if you are involved in an accident or breakdown, including the special arrangements for accidents or breakdowns on a motorway

5 basic first aid for use on the road as set out in *The Highway Code*

6 how to deter motorcycle thieves.

Motorway riding

You must gain a sound knowledge of the special rules, regulations and riding techniques for motorway riding before taking your riding test.

After passing your test, lessons are recommended with a motorcycle instructor before riding unsupervised on motorways.

DSA aims to give its customers the best possible service. Please tell us

- when we have done well
- when you aren't satisfied.

Your comments can help us to improve the service we offer. For information about DSA service standards, contact DSA Test Enquiries and Booking Centre 0870 01 01 372.

If you have any questions about how your test was conducted, please contact the local Supervising Examiner, whose address is displayed at your local driving test centre.

If you are dissatisfied with the reply or you wish to comment on other matters, you can write to

The Chief Executive
Driving Standards Agency
Stanley House
56 Talbot Street
Nottingham NG1 5GU

None of this removes your right to take your complaint to

- your Member of Parliament, who may decide to raise your case personally with the DSA Chief Executive, the Minister, or the Parliamentary Commissioner for Administration (the Ombudsman), whose name and address is at the back of this book
- a magistrates' court (in Scotland, to the Sheriff of your area) if you believe that your test wasn't carried out according to the regulations.

Before doing this, **you should seek legal advice.**

DSA always aims to keep test appointments, but occasionally we have to cancel a test at short notice. We will refund the test fee, or give you your next test free, in the following circumstances:

- if we cancel a test
- if you cancel a test and give us at least ten working days' notice
- if you keep the test appointment but the test doesn't take place or isn't finished, for a reason that isn't your fault or the fault of the motorcycle you are using.

We will also compensate you for the money you lost because we cancelled your test at short notice (unless it was for bad weather). For example, we will pay

- the cost of hiring a motorcycle for the test, including reasonable travelling time to and from the test centre
- any pay or earnings you lost, after tax and so on (usually for half a day).

We WON'T pay the cost of lessons which you arrange linked to a particular test appointment, or extra lessons you decide to take while waiting for a rescheduled test.

How to apply

Please write to the DSA Enquiries and Booking Centre and send a receipt showing hire charges, or an employer's letter which shows what earnings you lost. If possible, please use the standard form (available from every driving test centre or booking office) to make your claim.

These arrangements don't affect your legal rights.

DSA Test Enquiries and Booking Centre

DSA
PO Box 280
Newcastle-upon-Tyne
NE99 1FP

Tel: 0870 01 01 372

Welsh Speakers: 0870 01 00 372

Minicom: 0870 01 07 372

Fax: 0870 01 02 372

DSA Head Office

Stanley House
56 Talbot Street
Nottingham NG1 5GU

Tel: 0115 901 2500

Fax: 0115 901 2940

Other useful addresses

DETR Mobility Advice and Vehicle Information Service (MAVIS)

'O' Wing
MacAdam Avenue
Old Wokingham Road
Crowthorne
Berkshire RG45 6XD

Tel: 01344 661000

Fax: 01344 661066

Driver and Vehicle Licensing Agency (DVLA)

Customer Enquiry Unit
Swansea SA6 7JL

Tel: 01792 772151

Office of the Parliamentary Commissioner for Administration (The Parliamentary Ombudsman)

Millbank Tower
Millbank
London SW1P 4QP

Tel: 020 7217 4163

Fax: 020 7217 4160

You can use this log to record your progress through CBT. As you successfully complete each element get your instructor to sign this progress record. This will give you

- a record of when you successfully complete each element
- a record of your instructor
- evidence of your progress to date.

CBT training record

Name . . . .

has satisfactorily completed

Element A of CBT.   Signed . . . .   Date . . . .

Element B of CBT.   Signed . . . .   Date . . . .

Element C of CBT.   Signed . . . .   Date . . . .

Element D of CBT.   Signed . . . .   Date . . . .

Element E of CBT.   Signed . . . .   Date . . . .

for . . . . ATB

Essential Reading

The Highway Code

The Highway Code is essential reading for everyone. It explains road traffic law and gives guidance as to best driving practice, with particular reference to vulnerable road users such as horse riders, cyclists and the elderly. The current version was prepared to reflect the changes in lifestyle and technology, giving rules for dealing with driver fatigue and recommendations about the use of mobile phones.

0 11 552290 5   £1.49

Know Your Traffic Signs

This useful publication illustrates and explains the vast majority of traffic signals, signs and road markings which any road user is likely to encounter. It is the most comprehensive explanation of the signing system available, and is exceptional value for money.

0 11 551612 3   £2.50

Printed in The United Kingdom for The Stationery Office TJ003878   04/01   C50   63789

The Official Theory Test for Motorcyclists

A change to legislation from 1st February 2001 meant that anyone who wants to be eligible for a motorbike licence has to pass the motorcycle theory test before they do their practical motorcycle test. The change is part of the Government's road safety strategy to improve motorcycle safety.

The Official Theory Test for Motorcyclists contains the full question bank from which the questions for the motorbike theory test are taken.

ISBN 0 11 552223 9   £11.99

Motorcycle Riding – the essential skills

This new edition of *Motorcycle Riding – the essential skills* is the definitive guide for both novice and experienced riders, and is the essential reference manual for motorcycle instructors. Whether you're a new or an experienced rider, this book helps motorcyclists to acquire the skills needed to handle their machines correctly and keep them safe on the road.

ISBN 0 11 552257 3   £9.99

Order Form

5 easy ways to order:

- ● **Online:** Visit www.**clicktso**.com
- ○ **Tel:** Please call **0870 600 5522** *quoting ref BAW*
- ● **Fax:** Fax this form to **0870 600 5533**
- ● **Post:** **The Stationery Office, PO Box 29, Norwich NR3 1GN**
- ○ **TSO Bookshops:** Visit your local The Stationery Bookshop

---

Please send me the following publications:

Title	ISBN	Price	Quantity
The Highway Code	0 11 552290 5	£1.49	....
Know Your Traffic Signs	0 11 551612 3	£2.50	....
The Official Theory Test for Motorcyclists	0 11 552223 9	£11.99	....
Motorcycle Riding – the essential skills	0 11 552257 3	£9.99	....
Handling charge per order:		£3.00	
Total enclosed:		£.................	

PLEASE COMPLETE IN BLOCK CAPITALS

Name...

Address ....

....

....

.... Postcode .... | BAW |

☐ I enclose a cheque for £.................... payable to: *'The Stationery Office'*

☐ Please charge to my account with The Stationery Office, No:

....

☐ Please debit my Mastercard/Visa/Amex/Diners/Connect Card Account No.

Signature... Expiry date ....

☐ Please send me information on TSO products. My email address is

....@...

Alternatively, contact us NOW to register at www.**clicktso**.com

☐ Please tick this box if you do not wish to receive
further information by conventional mail on
products and services from The Stationery Office.

Prices are correct at time of going to press but may be
subject to change without notice.
TSO account holders should note that credit card
transactions will not be shown on their statements.
A full listing of terms and conditions of sale can be
obtained on request from The Stationery Office
PO Box 29, Norwich NR3 1GN.